Pray and Never Lose Heart

Pray and Never Lose Heart

The Power of Intercession

SR. ANN SHIELDS, S.G.L.

CHARIS

Servant Publications
Ann Arbor, Michigan

Charis Books is an imprint of Servant Publications especially designed to serve
Roman Catholics.

All Scriptures, unless otherwise indicated, are from the Revised Standard
Version of the Bible, copyrighted 1946, 1952, 1971 by the Division of Christian
Education of the National Council of Churches of Christ in the USA. Used by
permission. Verses marked NASB are from the New American Standard Bible,
© The Lockman Foundation 1960, 1962, 1963, 1968, 1971, 1972, 1973, 1975,
1977. Verses marked NAB are taken from the New American Bible. The Old
Testament of the New American Bible © 1970 by the Confraternity of Christian
Doctrine (CCD), Washington, D.C. (Books 1 Samuel to 2 Maccabees ©1969;
Revised New Testament of the New American Bible copyright ©1986 CCD;
Revised Psalms of the New American Bible copyright ©1991 CCD. All rights
reserved.

Published by Servant Publications
P.O. Box 8617
Ann Arbor, Michigan 48107

Cover design by Left Coast Design-Portland, OR

01 02 03 10 9 8 7 6 5 4 3 2 1

Printed in the United States of America
ISBN 0-56955-223-1

Contents

Contents

Acknowledgments

My heart rejoices in the motherly concern of Our Lady at Fatima, who taught us how necessary it is to pray for repentance and conversion—how prayer really does change things! May we be encouraged that we never pray alone; that he "who forever lives to make intercession for us" unites our prayer to his. The victory belongs to the Lord.

On the human and practical side of things, I owe a tremendous debt of gratitude to Gary Seromik who took so much of my teaching on intercession and transformed it from the spoken to the written word. Anyone who does editorial work knows the talent and skills required. May God and the intercession of his mother shower you, Gary, with the blessings of the faithful servant—the one who ultimately enters into the joy of your Lord—a joy no one will take from you!

Preface

Dear Brothers and Sisters,

I encourage you to read *Pray and Never Lose Heart* with a particular orientation in mind. Each chapter deals with some aspect of the Christian life or of spiritual growth, which can in turn make our intercession more effective, more fruitful.

This book is not a text on how to intercede or what to intercede for so much as it is on conforming our personal lives to Christ so our prayer can be heard. "The prayer of a righteous man [or woman] has great power in its effects" (James 5:16b, RSV).

Find the chapters that most identify where you are in your growth as a disciple. Focus there and the fruit will be, not only your growth in holiness, but effective prayer for others as well.

May God convict and inspire you,
Sr. Ann Shields

Introduction

In our society today it often seems as though faster equals better: instant money at ATM machines; fast food made even faster thanks to drive-thrus and microwaves; worldwide communication by cell phones, e-mail, and the Internet; and so on and so on. Inundated with such a mentality, we can approach our relationship with God, and specifically our intercession, with the same expectation of rapid results:

"I've asked God for a whole week and no answer. I guess he doesn't hear me or care about me or my needs....I've prayed and prayed for a year [insert your own time frame here], and things just get worse. Guess I don't have a gift for intercession, or God doesn't love me, or God must be deaf, or I'm too sinful."

You probably have your own particular reaction in such situations, but I think you see the point. We have been so "evangelized" by our culture that we forget the truth of who God is and how he acts:

> But do not ignore this one fact, beloved, that with the Lord one day is as a thousand years, and a thousand years as one day. The Lord is not slow about his promise as some count slowness, but is forbearing toward you, not wishing that any should perish, but that all should reach repentance.
>
> 2 PETER 3:8-9

For a thousand years in thy sight are but as yesterday when it is past, or as a watch in the night.

PSALM 90:4

For my thoughts are not your thoughts, neither are your ways my ways, says the Lord. For as the heavens are higher than the earth, so are my ways higher than your ways and my thoughts than your thoughts. For as the rain and the snow come down from heaven, and return not thither but water the earth, making it bring forth and sprout, giving seed to the sower and bread to the eater, so shall my word be that goes forth from my mouth; it shall not return to me empty but it shall accomplish that which I purpose and prosper in the thing for which I sent it.

ISAIAH 55:8-11

And most notably, Jesus tells us, "Whatever you ask in my name, I will do" (Jn 14:13). How do we enter into the fulfillment of this promise?

This book is the fruit of learning how to pray according to God's mind and how to allow my prayer to reflect his infinite mercy. *There are no formulas.* Intercession depends, in large part, upon our commitment to daily growth in our relationship with God, a love relationship that encompasses him and his people. It entails acknowledgement of our sin and death to that sin, as well as a commitment to discipleship and obedience to his word. We may stumble on this path, but as we repent, God reveals to us his heart of mercy and love. Then we are able to more faithfully and confidently pray in his name.

The Message of Fatima

Over the past year I have found strength in the message God asked Our Lady to give us through three young children in Portugal in 1917. A part of the children's vision has encouraged me particularly in intercession. I am taking the liberty of quoting extensively from Cardinal Joseph Ratzinger's and Cardinal Angelo Sodano's theological commentary on the visions of Fatima. The explanation should inspire everyone who is engaged in the ministry of intercession. (For the entire text, please see *Origins*, Vol. 30, No. 8, July 6, 2000.)

"Well, the secret is made up of three distinct parts, two of which I am now going to reveal.

"The first part is the vision of hell.

"Our Lady showed us a great sea of fire which seemed to be under the earth. Plunged in this fire were demons and souls in human form, like transparent burning embers, all blackened or burnished bronze, floating about in the conflagration, now raised into the air by the flames that issued from within themselves together with great clouds of smoke, now falling back on every side like sparks in a huge fire, without weight or equilibrium, amid shrieks and groans of pain and despair, which horrified us and made us tremble with fear. The demons could be distinguished by their terrifying and repulsive likeness to frightful and unknown animals, all black and transparent. This vision lasted but an instant. How can we ever be grateful enough to our kind heavenly Mother, who had already prepared us by promising, in the first apparition, to take us to heaven. Otherwise, I think we would have died of fear and terror.

"We then looked up at Our Lady, who said to us so kindly and so sadly:

"'You have seen hell where the souls of poor sinners go. To save them, God wishes to establish in the world devotion to my Immaculate Heart. If what I say to you is done, many souls will be saved and there will be peace. The war is going to end. But if people do not cease offending God, a worse one will break out during the pontificate of Pius XI. When you see a night illumined by an unknown light, know that this is a great sign given you by God that he is about to punish the world for its crimes, by means of war, famine, and persecutions of the church and of the Holy Father. To prevent this, I shall come to ask for the consecration of Russia to my Immaculate Heart, and the communion of reparation on the First Saturdays. If my requests are heeded, Russia will be converted, and there will be peace; if not, she will spread her errors throughout the world, causing wars and persecutions of the church. The good will be martyred; the Holy Father will have much to suffer; various nations will be annihilated. In the end, my Immaculate Heart will triumph. The Holy Father will consecrate Russia to me, and she shall be converted, and a period of peace will be granted to the world.'

"The third part of the secret revealed at the Cova da Iria-Fatima, on July 13, 1917. [Vatican-approved text, translated from the handwritten Portuguese text.]

"After the two parts which I have already explained, at the left of Our Lady and a little above, we saw an angel with a flaming sword in his left hand; flashing, it gave out flames that looked as though they would set the world on fire, but they died out in contact with the splendor that Our Lady radiated toward him from her right hand. Pointing to the earth with his right hand, the angel cried out in a loud voice: 'Penance, penance, penance!' And we saw, in an immense light that is God, something similar to how people appear in a mirror when they pass in front of it, a bishop dressed in white—we had the impression that it was the Holy Father. [We saw} other bishops, priests, men and women religious going up a steep mountain, at the top of which there was a big cross of rough-hewn trunks as of a cork tree with the bark; before reaching there the Holy Father passed through a big city half in ruins. Half-trembling with halting step, afflicted with pain and sorrow, he prayed for the souls of the corpses he met on his way. Having reached the top of the mountain, on his knees at the foot of the big cross, he was killed by a group of soldiers who fired bullets and arrows at him, and in the same way there died, one after another, the other bishops, priests, men and women religious, and various lay people of different ranks and positions. Beneath the two arms of the cross there were two angels each with a crystal aspersorium in his hand, in which they gathered up the blood of the martyrs and with it sprinkled the souls that were making their way to God.

"The first and second parts of the 'secret' of Fatima have already been so amply discussed in the relative literature that there is no need to deal with them again here. I would just like to recall briefly the most significant point. For one terrible moment, the children were given a vision of hell. They saw the fall of 'the souls of poor sinners.' And now they are told why they have been exposed to this moment: 'in order to save souls'—to show the way to salvation. The words of the First Letter of Peter come to mind: 'As the outcome of your faith you obtain the salvation of your souls' (1:9). To reach this goal, the way indicated—surprisingly for people from the Anglo-Saxon and German cultural world—is devotion to the Immaculate Heart of Mary. A brief comment may suffice to explain this.

"In biblical language, the 'heart' indicates the center of human life, the point where reason, will, temperament, and sensitivity converge, where the person finds his unity and his interior orientation. According to Matthew 5:8, the 'immaculate heart' is a heart which, with God's grace, has come to perfect interior unity and therefore 'sees God.' To be 'devoted' to the Immaculate Heart of Mary means therefore to embrace this attitude of heart, which makes the *fiat*—'Your will be done'—the defining center of one's whole life. It might be objected that we should not place a human being between ourselves and Christ. But then we remember that Paul did not hesitate to say to his communities: 'Imitate me' (1 Cor 4:16; Phil 3:17; 1 Thes 1:6; 2 Thes 3:7, 9). In the Apostle they could see concretely what it meant to follow Christ. But from whom might we better learn in every age than from the Mother of the Lord?

"Thus we come finally to the third part of the 'secret' of Fatima which for the first time is being published in its entirety. As is clear from the documentation presented here, the interpretation offered by Cardinal Sodano in his statement of 13 May was first put personally to Sister Lucia. Sister Lucia responded by pointing out that she had received the vision but not its interpretation. The interpretation, she said, belonged not to the visionary but to the Church. After reading the text, however, she said that this interpretation corresponded to what she had experienced and that on her part she thought the interpretation correct. In what follows, therefore, we can only attempt to provide a deeper foundation for this interpretation, on the basis of the criteria already considered.

"'To save souls' has emerged as the key word of the first and second parts of the 'secret,' and the key word of this third part is the threefold cry: 'Penance, Penance, Penance!' The beginning of the Gospel comes to mind: 'Repent and believe the Good News' (Mk 1:15). To understand the signs of the times means to accept the urgency of penance—of conversion—of faith. This is the correct response to this moment of history, characterized by the grave perils outlined in the images that follow.

"Allow me to add here a personal recollection: in a conversation with me, Sister Lucia said that it appeared ever more clearly to her that the purpose of all the apparitions was to help people to grow more and more in faith, hope, and love—everything else was intended to lead to this.

"Let us now examine more closely the single images. The angel with the flaming sword on the left of the Mother of God recalls similar images in the Book of Revelation. This represents the threat of judgment which looms over the world. Today the prospect that the world might be reduced to ashes by a sea of fire no longer seems pure fantasy: man himself, with his inventions, has forged the flaming sword. The vision then shows the power which stands opposed to the force of destruction—the splendor of the Mother of God and, stemming from this in a certain way, the summons to penance. In this way, the importance of human freedom is underlined: the future is not in fact unchangeably set, and the image which the children saw is in no way a film preview of a future in which nothing can be changed. Indeed, the whole point of the vision is to bring freedom onto the scene and to steer freedom in a positive direction.

"The purpose of the vision is not to show a film of an irrevocably fixed future. Its meaning is exactly the opposite: it is meant to mobilize the forces of change in the right direction. Therefore we must totally discount fatalistic explanations of the 'secret,' such as, for example, the claim that the would-be assassin of 13 May 1981 was merely an instrument of the divine plan guided by Providence and could not therefore have acted freely, or other similar ideas in circulation. Rather, the vision speaks of dangers and how we might be saved from them.

"The next phrases of the text show very clearly once again the symbolic character of the vision: God remains immeasurable, and is the light which surpasses every vision of ours. Human persons appear as in a mirror. We must always keep in mind the limits in the vision itself, which here are indicated visually. The future appears only 'in a mirror dimly' (1 Cor 13:12). Let us now consider the individual images which follow in the text of the 'secret.' The place of the action is described in three symbols: a steep mountain, a great city reduced to ruins, and finally a large rough-hewn cross. The mountain and city symbolize the arena of human history: history as an arduous ascent to the summit, history as the arena of human creativity and social harmony, but at the same time a place of destruction, where man actually destroys the fruits of his own work. The city can be the place of communion and progress, but also of danger and the most extreme menace. On the mountain stands the cross—the goal and guide of history. The cross transforms destruction into salvation; it stands as a sign of history's misery but also as a promise for history.

"At this point human persons appear: the Bishop dressed in white ('We had the impression that it was the Holy Father'), other bishops, priests, men and women religious, and men and women of different ranks and social positions. The Pope seems to precede the others, trembling and suffering because of all the horrors around him. Not only do the houses of the city lie half in ruins, but he makes his way among the corpses of the dead. The Church's path is thus described as a *Via Crucis*, as a journey through a time of violence, destruction, and persecution. The history of an entire century can be seen represented in this image.

"Just as the places of the earth are synthetically described in the two images of the mountain and the city, and are directed towards the cross, so too time is presented in a compressed way. In the vision we can recognize the last century as a century of martyrs, a century of suffering and persecution for the Church, a century of World Wars and the many local wars which filled the last fifty years and have inflicted unprecedented forms of cruelty. In the 'mirror' of this vision we see passing before us the witnesses of the faith decade by decade. Here it would be appropriate to mention a phrase from the letter which Sister Lucia wrote to the Holy Father on 12 May 1982: 'The third part of the "secret" refers to Our Lady's words: "If not, [Russia] will spread her errors throughout the world, causing wars and persecutions of the Church. The good will be martyred; the Holy Father will have much to suffer; various nations will be annihilated."'

"In the *Via Crucis* of an entire century, the figure of the Pope has a special role. In his arduous ascent of the mountain we can undoubtedly see a convergence of different Popes. Beginning from Pius X up to the present Pope, they all shared the sufferings of the century and strove to go forward through all the anguish along the path which leads to the cross. In the vision, the Pope too is killed along with the martyrs.

"When, after the attempted assassination on 13 May 1981, the Holy Father had the text of the third part of the 'secret' brought to him, was it not inevitable that he should see in it his own fate? He had been very close to death, and he himself explained his survival in the following words: 'It was a mother's hand that guided the bullet's path and in his throes the Pope halted at the threshold of death' (13 May 1994). That here 'a mother's hand' had deflected the fateful bullet only shows once more that there is no immutable destiny, that faith and prayer are forces which can influence history and that in the end prayer is more powerful than bullets and faith more powerful than armies."

CHAPTER 1

THE POWER OF THE SACRAMENTS

*T*he focus and goal of everything I write here is to bring us to the grace, the gift, of a devoted heart—which in God's will is the center of one's whole life. As we put our feet more and more firmly on that path, our prayers will be heard.

As we begin, it is essential for each of us to see and to rely on all the help we have been given. Let us look first at the sacraments: baptism, confirmation, penance, Eucharist, and matrimony. The sacraments are the primary means the Lord has given us in order to share his divine life with us. He has given them not only to sanctify us but also to build up the body of Christ and to give worship to God. The sacraments nourish and strengthen our faith; they also express that faith.

Baptism

When you and I were baptized, God himself came to take up residence in us:

What shall we say then? Are we to continue in sin that grace may abound? By no means! How can we who died to sin still live in it? Do you not know that all of us who have been baptized into Christ Jesus were baptized into his death? We were buried therefore with him by baptism into death, so that as Christ was raised from the dead by the glory of the Father, we too might walk in newness of life. For if we have been united with him in a death like his, we shall certainly be united with him in a resurrection like his. We know that our old self was crucified with him so that the sinful body might be destroyed, and we might no longer be enslaved to sin.

ROMANS 6:1-6

For purposes of clarity, imagine a circle in your mind:

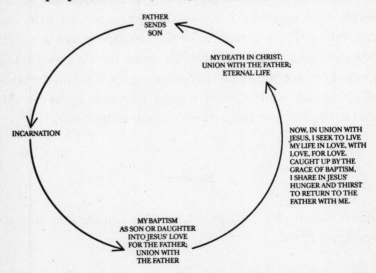

All your life, since your baptism, Jesus is, so to speak, longing to return to the Father through you:

I do not pray for these only, but also for those who believe in me through their word, that they may all be one; even as thou, Father, art in me, and I in thee, that they also may be in us, so that the world may believe that thou hast sent me. The glory which thou hast given me I have given to them, that they may be one even as we are one. I in them and thou in me, that they may become perfectly one, so that the world may know that thou hast sent me and hast loved them even as thou hast loved me. Father, I desire that they also, whom thou hast given me, may be with me where I am, to behold my glory, which thou hast given me in thy love for me before the foundation of the world. O righteous Father, the world has not known thee, but I have known thee; and these know that thou hast sent me. I made known to them thy name, and I will make it known that the love with which thou hast loved me may be in them, and I in them.

JOHN 17:20-26

You are living out, as a daughter or a son, the love that Jesus has for the Father and the Father has for the Son. Stop and ponder that for a moment. It is breathtaking. You are loved as much and in the same way as the Father loves the Son and the Son loves the Father. Your baptism really changed you. Your life is now immortal; your inheritance is eternal. You have full access to the Father through Jesus. The writer of the Letter to the Hebrews tells us that Jesus "always lives to make intercession" for us (Heb 7:25). That prayer is going on *in us* by God's Spirit all the time, as long as we are in a state of grace.

Our "job," so to speak, is to tap into that prayer and that love by our relationship as a son or daughter. If we surrender-our lives to that relationship, we can know with confidence that our prayer, united with Jesus, will be heard before the throne of God. That is the kind of access to God that we have through our baptism.

I have a word here for godparents: When you pray for those people for whom you accepted responsibility at the time of their baptism, call on the graces of their baptism and your baptism, of their confirmation and your confirmation. God will hear your prayer. But at the same time and in complete trust, you must leave the way and the timing to the One who is all Love.

Confirmation

Confirmation brings us more gifts, and it brings to maturity the gifts God gave us in baptism. This lavish grace always presumes our cooperation. We should all take a moment from time to time to read and ponder what confirmation offers us. Look at the gifts. One list is found in Isaiah 11:2-3:

And the spirit of the Lord shall rest upon him,
the spirit of wisdom and understanding,
the spirit of counsel and might,
the spirit of knowledge and the fear of the Lord.
And his delight shall be in the fear of the Lord.

These are gifts by which we, as sons and daughters, participate and share in the very *mind* and *heart* of our Father by the power of the Spirit. This sacrament should enable us to "take

Serenity

The world is always rushing by.
Time passes before us
in the blink of an eye.
In the midst of it all
we try to keep our bearing.
We center our hearts,
on faith, love and caring.

We pray for serenity, Lord,
a little peace of mind.
Focus our scattered thoughts,
calm our restless spirits,
slow down this race
against time.

Photo credit: Bro. John E. Argauer, M.M.

Maryknoll Fathers and Brothers
PO Box 302, Maryknoll, New York 10545-0302
888-627-9566
Visit our website at: www.maryknoll.org

on," so to speak, the family likeness, the family mind and heart, the family way of thinking and acting.

St. Paul, in 1 Corinthians 12, gives us an explanation of spiritual gifts meant particularly to be used by us as servants of God to build up the body of Christ. As adult Christians, as full members of the Church, we are given these treasures for our own holiness and for the sanctification and evangelization of everyone. These graces empower us to intercede.

But take note: The power is *God's*. It is our duty to surrender to his will, in his way, in his time, in the use of these gifts. We are the servants; he is the Master. There is no room for pride or ambition. It is all a matter of relationship, of God's love for us and how we can extend that love to others.

Penance

Jesus, the divine physician of both our bodies and our souls, has provided for our ongoing healing and salvation through the sacrament of penance. When we fail in daily life—and we will fail very often—this sacrament is there so we might grow in humility, experience God's mercy, and go forth in that mercy to pray for others and serve them.

The sacrament of penance is a powerful intervention of God's mercy in our lives. God says: "I am he who blots out your transgressions for my own sake, and I will not remember your sins" (Is 43:25). And: "I have swept away your transgressions like a cloud and your sins like a mist" (Is 44:22). When God forgives, he forgets, and our sins disappear like the mist.

This total forgiveness is contrary to our sinful, human

behavior. Let's admit it. When we forgive, we often say to ourselves, "I forgive you, but don't let it happen again." When it does happen again, we usually respond by saying, "Do you remember when you ...?" When we forgive, it takes tremendous grace to forget. We can do so only with the power of God's grace.

Through regular confession God's love can touch the deep, dark recesses of our hearts—including those that we do not know exist. The more we repent, the more our eyes, our ears, and our hearts are opened to see the roots of sin in our lives. Just as rainwater penetrates the earth so the soil can bear fruit, the life of Christ permeates our lives and changes us through the sacrament of penance. I have noticed that the more I go to confession, the more I experience strength to turn away from sin and to pursue what is good and holy.

When we begin to take this sacrament seriously, a good spiritual director will oftentimes help us uncover areas in our lives where we are harboring resentment, hurts, or anxieties. Sometimes these problems are the result of some unfortunate circumstances in our lives. If we are able to uncover the root of these problems, we can invite the Lord to enter into these areas to bring about change within us.

Besides being a powerful tool for pardon, reconciliation, and inner healing, the sacrament of penance can also be a tool for intercession. Our sins touch the lives of those around us. They separate us from God but also from one another. We need to ask forgiveness for our sin; we also need to pray for those people whom we have offended. Then the powerful grace that we receive in the sacrament is released and touches their lives.

Many individuals have shared with me how they have

harbored feelings of resentment toward a parent, a sibling, or another family member. Most commonly they would describe these relationships as "all messed up." Although the situation bothered them, they figured that it was not their fault and there was little they could do. Yet, invariably, once they confessed their feelings in the confessional, their eyes were opened to the ways in which their own selfishness and lack of charity contributed to the problem. They were able to ask God to work in that situation. Over time many have witnessed radical changes in these relationships; others, especially in cases where the family member was already deceased, experienced a tremendous peace as they interceded for that person.

The Eucharist

Lumen Gentium describes the Eucharist as "the source and summit of the Christian life." What a privilege we have to share this intimate union with our Savior! Through the Eucharist Christ permits us mere human beings to carry within our mortal bodies his body, blood, soul, and divinity. In many ways this is tantamount to the privilege that God granted to Mary when he chose her to bear his Son. Even the angels in heaven look upon us with envy because God has granted us a privilege that they do not share.

I do not know how we, as intercessors, can live a spiritual life that bears great fruit (including having our prayers answered) unless we are feeding on the life that God intended us to feed on. The Eucharist is essential to our life. It is food for the soul; it is food for life eternal.

Many people tell me, "I've prayed and prayed for this intention without any results." They are often discouraged, depressed, and angry with God. As I probe deeper, I often find that they are not feeding on Jesus, the veritable Source of Life who could help them! I urge everyone to take a look at the place that the Eucharist occupies in your life.

Make a special effort to truly understand and embrace the Church's teaching on the Eucharist. To anyone who wishes to grow in appreciation of this sacrament, I particularly recommend Scott Hahn's book *The Supper of the Lamb*. Ask God to give you faith or to increase your faith in the Eucharist—and he will do it.

The Eucharist is the highest form of worship; it is also the highest form of intercession when we fully participate in it and offer it for our needs and the needs of others. Indeed, if we give our burdens and cares to the Lord during Mass, we can trust him to show us—and those for whom we pray—his way and his will. We can receive his vision, and grow in faith, hope, and love.

Throughout the Mass we intercede for various needs. During the Prayers of the Faithful we pray for those needs that are especially relevant at the time, whether it be the victims of war, flood, or famine, or individuals in our parish community who are sick. During the Liturgy of the Eucharist, in the Canon, every day, we intercede for both the living and the dead in union with Jesus who forever lives to make intercession for us. Finally, every time a priest celebrates the Eucharist, he offers it for a particular intention. As intercessors, we should take these intentions to heart and pray along with the priest for them.

Come to the well, daily if possible. The Eucharist will nourish you and sustain you, so you can walk as a daughter or son of God, more and more in love with Christ, more and more in union with his will.

Matrimony

The sacraments of holy orders and matrimony are directed not only toward the individual's personal salvation but also to building up the people of God. Husbands and wives, grandparents, as you pray for your children and grandchildren, draw on your marriage covenant. The sacrament of marriage is not a one-day, one-time thing. Since the moment you were married, the grace of the sacrament has been flowing, not only for you but for your spouse, your children, your entire family. The more you can be on your knees together, opening yourselves to new and powerful graces of that sacrament, the more you will see God's abundant provision. When your spouse, your children, your grandchildren are in difficulty, call on the power of the sacrament for wisdom, for unity, for courage. God will supply!

As the Lord told St. Paul, "My grace is sufficient for you, for my power is made perfect in weakness" (2 Cor 12:9). Likewise, St. Paul assures us: "My God will supply every need of yours according to his riches in Christ Jesus" (Phil 4:19).

We don't call enough on the treasures God has placed at our disposal through the sacraments. We need to! Our families are so much in crisis today. God will not abandon us, but we need to turn to him in faith. That kind of trust is rewarded.

CHAPTER 2

INTERCEDING AS CHILDREN OF GOD

"Father, hallowed be thy name. Thy kingdom come. Give us each day our daily bread; and forgive us our sins, for we ourselves forgive every one who is indebted to us; and lead us not into temptation."

LUKE 11:2-4

*A*nother natural starting point for any study of prayer and intercession is the prayer that Jesus himself gave us: "The Our Father" or "The Lord's Prayer." It is the first prayer most of us learn, the prayer we pray most often, and, unfortunately, the prayer we usually rattle off without much thought.

When we read "The Lord's Prayer" in the Gospels, we get a fresh look at this almost too familiar prayer. For one thing, the wording is a little different, especially here in the Gospel of Luke, which gives a shorter version of Jesus' prayer than the Gospel of Matthew. Just the difference of a few words can be enough to break the haze of familiarity and help us hear what Jesus is really saying.

Even more important, however, is the way the Gospels set "The Lord's Prayer" in the context of Jesus' broader teaching on prayer. After all, Jesus was not trying to make sure that we would always pray in exactly the same words. He was giving us a model for prayer, a lesson in how to pray. He was teaching us basic truths about our relationship with God, starting with the key truth that God is our Father.

An Intimate Relationship

Praying to God as Father was not a brand-new idea with Jesus. In the Old Testament we find other examples: "For thou art our Father...our Redeemer from of old is thy name" (Is 63:16), and, "Because he is our Lord and God, he is our Father for ever" (Tb 13:4). Yet nowhere in the Old Testament do we find the sense of intimacy and total unity that marked Jesus' relationship with his Father. Only Jesus could say, "I and the Father are one" (Jn 10:30) and again, "The Father is in me and I am in the Father" (Jn 10:38; 14:10).

When Jesus teaches us to address God as Father, he invites us into his own intimate relationship with his Father. In Jesus we become children of God, not just in the broad sense that God is the ultimate source of our life but in the very specific, unique sense of sonship that we see in Jesus. "So through God you are no longer a slave but a son," the apostle Paul tells us, "and if a son then an heir" (Gal 4:7).

Anytime we turn to God in prayer, and especially when we are interceding for others, we come to him as children approaching a beloved Father. We can put our prayers before God with the same confidence Jesus had: "Father, I thank thee that thou hast heard me. I knew that thou hearest me always" (Jn 11:41-42).

Unfortunately, many people today fail to grasp the concept of what it means to be a father. Oftentimes they even have a negative concept of the word. Some were abused, while others were abandoned by their fathers. And many more simply did not have good, loving fathers. Yet, even if our relationship with our earthly father was inadequate, and even if we require counseling and ministry in this area, we need to focus on what our heavenly Father offers us. *Spiritually* we are not orphans. On the contrary, we have the most loving Father in the whole universe and beyond. We have a Father who is in heaven. Moreover, our heavenly Father wants to reveal himself to us.

The Father's Care

I myself had a very good human father, for which I am deeply grateful. So I was surprised a number of years ago, just before leaving for a trip to Australia, when I sensed that the Lord was speaking to me about this area. (It was not an audible voice but a thought that came into my mind as I was praying. Sometimes these thoughts are merely our own thoughts, but they are often inspirations from the Holy Spirit.) I felt that the Lord wanted to show me that he was a loving Father who cares about our every need. And I felt that he wanted to teach me this in the course of my trip.

I did not object, of course. It certainly would be a blessing to experience God's love for me in some way. Yet, since this word did not correspond to any particular need I had at the time, I didn't think much about it as I hurriedly made the final preparations for my trip.

I was traveling with several other people. Our itinerary took us from Pennsylvania to California, then to Australia, and finally to New Zealand. Between California and Australia, we had a two-hour fuel stop in Tahiti, a beautiful island in the

South Pacific. Ten minutes after we took off from there, the pilot announced that the plane was having serious mechanical problems. He would have to jettison most of the plane's fuel as he attempted to land in Tahiti once again.

I immediately realized that we were in serious trouble. I knew very well that the pilot of an aircraft jettisons the plane's fuel only when it is in danger of a crash landing. Looking out the window, I watched the fuel as it was being dumped. Fr. Michael Scanlan was seated next to me. He looked at me and asked, "Are you ready?"

I had gone to confession the preceding day, and I told him I honestly thought I was ready. Nevertheless, I admitted that I was scared. Then I asked him, "Are you ready?"

"I think so," he replied. "Let's pray the Lord's Prayer together out loud."

Fr. Scanlan began to pray, "Our Father, who art in heaven ..." Everybody on the plane chimed in, each in his own language. Then there was silence. No one was hysterical; no one was crying. The flight attendants prepared us for a crash landing. Fortunately, we landed safely in Tahiti. Nine hours later we were told that the plane was fixed and that we would be able to continue on our trip. Needless to say, it was truly a challenge to my faith to get back on the same plane!

After that experience I prayed, "Lord, thank you for providing for me. Thank you for being such a good Father to me. Thank you." I thought that this was the lesson that the Lord had wanted to teach me—the sense that he had given to me before leaving on the trip.

His Promise Is True

We arrived in Australia, and we spoke at a series of conferences around the country. When the conferences were over, we gathered in the lobby of the hotel for the drive to the airport. Fr. Scanlan and I were scheduled to continue on to New Zealand, so I asked him if he had our tickets. Suddenly he remembered that the tickets were back in the hotel room he had just vacated.

One of the men who had shared a room with him offered to go up to the room and get the tickets. About five minutes later he came back and announced, "They have a very efficient maid service in this hotel. The maid thought they were used tickets and threw them down the trash chute."

Once again the Lord's promise to me popped into my mind: "I want to show you what a loving Father you have, a Father who knows your every need."

"Well, what do we do?" I asked.

"I could advance you the money," our host offered. "It would probably be three or four thousand dollars."

I was hesitant to take him up on his offer. I was somewhat familiar with the problems entailed with lost tickets, and I knew it would take three to six months for him to get his money back. Furthermore, it was a Saturday afternoon, and the travel agencies were closed. We had to speak in New Zealand on Sunday.

We found the hotel manager and asked him if there was any way we could search for the tickets in the trash. He did not offer much hope, but he told us we were welcome to speak with the maintenance man in the basement of the hotel. So the entire group trooped down to the basement. There we met the maintenance man, who led us to a brick room where the incinerator was located. (It reminded me of the fiery furnace in the Book of Daniel, where King Nebuchadnezzar threw the three young men, Shadrach, Meshach, and Abednego.)

The maintenance man pointed to a trapdoor in the ceiling. "You see that trapdoor up there?" he said. "I pull that trapdoor, and down comes all the trash from that chute. I haven't pulled that trapdoor since four o'clock yesterday afternoon."

At this point everyone in our party was backing out the door, thanking him for his help. It was a large hotel, and the quantity of trash that had accumulated would not only be enormous but messy as well! But once again I remembered the Lord's words to me, so I sheepishly asked him, "Would you just pull it once?"

I felt as though I were speaking in spite of myself. I, too, wanted to back out of such a forbidding room. The man looked at me, then pulled the trapdoor. A huge quantity of paper trash descended onto the floor of the furnace. Then he took a rake and started to rake the debris, stirring up the coals as he raked. Little by little, flames began to flicker and grow. Everyone was silent.

The flames grew higher. I stood there looking into the furnace and saying to myself, "Father, you promised." At that moment two tickets descended, seemingly from nowhere since the trapdoor had already sprung shut. Moreover, they did not land in the flames but on a ledge that was directly in front of me. At first I thought, "They can't be ours." But when I picked them up and looked at them, I realized they indeed were our tickets!

Normally I am not very demonstrative when it comes to expressing my emotions. But I bounded up the stairs with those tickets and jumped around the lobby crying out, "Praise God for these tickets!" I spotted the manager of the hotel and told him the whole story. "There is nothing else to say but praise the Lord!" he replied.

The word that the Lord had spoken to me before the trip, "I want to show you what a loving Father you have," continued to resound in my mind. I knew then and there beyond a shadow of a doubt that God's word is true. I recalled the words of the psalmist: "For thou didst form my inward parts, thou didst knit me together in my mother's womb" (Ps 139:13).

Up to that point the Lord had not often answered my prayers the way I would have liked him to answer them. And even since then the Lord has not always answered my prayers the way I would like him to answer them. Yet I continue to cling to this memory as a marvelous reminder of God's personal love for me—a love so great that he sent us his only begotten Son to die on the cross for our salvation, and then displayed it in such a practical, homespun way.

If, for some reason, you do not believe you have such a loving Father, ask God to reveal himself to you. Ask the Father to manifest himself to you, and he will do so. He longs to make himself known.

He Knows Us

I always thought that the above incident was an excellent illustration of God's personal love and concern for each and every one of us. Then, several years ago a good friend, who knows that I relish stories that illustrate spiritual truths, called me with a story he had just heard. "Now I really have a story for you," he said. "This one is absolutely verified."

He then proceeded to tell me a story about Ken Gaub, a church pastor who also had a television ministry. Later I learned that Rev. Ken Gaub had recounted this story, among others, in a book he had written called *God's Got Your Number* (New Leaf Press, P.O. Box 311, Green Forest, AR 72638, 1986). In fact, he kindly sent me a copy of his book when he heard that I often shared his story in my talks.

From all appearances, things were going fine for Pastor Gaub. Nonetheless, inwardly he felt trapped in a "self-induced cocoon of despondency." As he described it, "A melancholy cloud of self-pity enshrouded my mind.... I seemed to have used up all my faith in ministering to others."

When he was in the midst of this time of discouragement, he and his wife, Barbara, were traveling across the United States with their children. When they were on I-75 near Dayton, Ohio, they decided to pull off the road and take a break at a pizza parlor. Ken decided that he was not feeling hungry, so he asked his wife to take the kids inside while he rested.

That day he was feeling particularly down. "God, even a preacher needs to know that you are aware of him once in a while," he pleaded inside. Feeling antsy, he noticed a Dairy Queen down the street and decided that he was thirsty and that a walk would do him some good. After purchasing a Coke, he was walking back to the pizza parlor when he heard the impatient ringing of a telephone coming from a phone booth at a gas station on the corner.

At first he thought the call must be for one of the employees at the gas station, so he ignored it. Then he realized that the gas station attendant continued to look after his customers, oblivious to the incessant ringing. "It may be important," he reasoned. "What if it's an emergency?" Finally, out of both curiosity and irritation, he went over and picked up the phone.

"Long-distance call for Ken Gaub," the operator said. Immediately he thought it was a set-up: "I know what this is! I'm on *Candid Camera!*" he thought. Looking into the glass of the phone booth, he started smoothing his hair so he would look his best for all the millions of television viewers. At the same time, he was searching for a hidden camera.

Impatiently the operator interrupted again. "I have a long-distance call for Ken Gaub, sir. Is he there?"

Shaken and perplexed, he asked, "How in the world can this be? How did you reach me here? I was walking down the street, not bothering anyone, the pay phone started ringing, and I decided to answer it. I just answered it on chance. You can't mean me. This is impossible!"

Finally the operator was able to convince him that it was not a joke. When he realized that there was indeed a call for him on the line, his heart began to pound. "Yes, that's him, operator. I believe that's him," he heard a faint voice say in the background.

Ken was dumbfounded when the caller identified herself. "Ken Gaub, I'm Millie from Harrisburg, Pennsylvania. You don't know me, but I'm desperate. Please help me."

The woman explained that she had been in the middle of writing a suicide note when she began to pray. She told God that she really did not want to commit suicide. "I suddenly remembered seeing you on television and thought if I could just talk to you, you could help me," she said. She continued writing her suicide note, since she could see no way out of her situation, but numbers started to come to her mind. She scribbled them down.

"I looked at those numbers and thought, 'Wouldn't it be wonderful if I had a miracle from God, and he has given me Ken's phone number?'" So she decided to try, figuring it was worth the chance.

"Are you in your office?" she asked. (His office was located in Yakima, Washington.)

"Ma'am, you won't believe this," he said, "but I'm in a phone booth in Dayton, Ohio!"

Knowing that this encounter could only have been arranged by God, he got down on his knees right there in the phone booth. He prayed with this woman and counseled her. It was a powerful moment of grace for her and for him.

"I walked away from that telephone booth with an electrifying sense of our heavenly Father's concern for each of his children. I was astonished as I thought of the astronomical odds of this happening. With all the millions of phones and innumerable combinations of numbers, only an all-knowing God could have caused that woman to call that number in that phone booth at that moment in time."

Bursting with exhilaration, he could not contain his story. He found his wife and blurted out, "Barb, you won't believe this! God knows where I am!"

She replied, "Of course God does."

"No," he countered, "He *really* knows right where I am."

That is as true for you as for Pastor Gaub. God knows where

we are each and every moment of the day. We have a Father who loves us and who is watching over us. He knows our problems. He knows what we face spiritually, physically, emotionally, and financially.

Abundant Life

At one time or another we all have heard a teaching on "The Prosperity Gospel." According to this teaching, if we follow the Lord and if we give ourselves to him, we will experience blessing upon blessing. I personally believe that this is true spiritually though not necessarily materially.

Scripture does not tell us that God will remove all human trial and suffering. We need only to look at our Lord Jesus Christ, the Virgin Mary, and St. Joseph—the people nearest to the Father—to realize this. Did they go through life without difficulties? On the contrary, they all had to face various trials and sufferings. For this reason, it is important that we never equate suffering with abandonment, rejection, or punishment from God. Scripture is very clear: "He delivers the afflicted by their affliction, and opens their ear by adversity" (Jb 36:15). We need to trust that God, our Father, is here with us now and loves each and every one of us.

In John 3:16 we read: "For God so loved the world that he gave his only Son, that whoever believes in him should not perish but have eternal life." God gave us his Son, Jesus Christ, to save us because he wants us to share in his life for all eternity.

When my father was dying, he used to say to me over and

over, "Honey, talk to me about heaven. Nobody talks about heaven. Where am I going?"

I used to read him passages from the Gospel of John where Jesus talked about going before us to prepare a place for us. I also read him passages from the Book of Revelation, which I love, especially those passages that describe what the new heavens and the new earth will be like. I particularly liked to read over and over Revelation 21:3-5:

> *"Behold, the dwelling of God is with men. He will dwell with them, and they shall be his people, and God himself will be with them; he will wipe away every tear from their eyes, and death shall be no more, neither shall there be mourning nor crying nor pain any more, for the former things have passed away." And he who sat upon the throne said, "Behold I make all things new." Also he said, "Write this, for these words are trustworthy and true."*

St. Paul reminds us that, even though we cannot begin to comprehend what awaits us in heaven, the Holy Spirit can work in our lives to reveal something about the eternal life that awaits us: "But, as it is written, 'What no eye has seen, nor ear heard, nor the heart of man conceived, what God has prepared for those who love him,' God has revealed to us through the Spirit. For the Spirit searches everything, even the depths of God" (1 Cor 2:9-10). He tells as well something about a Father who so loves us that he sent his Son—a Son who so loved the Father that he would do anything the Father wanted—to suffer and die for us, that we might inherit life with him forever.

For this reason, I always recommend a practice that I have made a habit over the years. Take a moment from time to time to think about the most beautiful and the best that you have ever seen or experienced in your life. Likewise, take a moment to think about a time when you really encountered unequivocal love. When you do so, these moments will give you a pale, tiny glimmer of what heaven is like. You will have a glimpse of what it will be like when you will be forever in the presence of the One who is all love, all beauty, all truth, and all goodness.

An eternal perspective sheds light and purpose on our earthly trials.

Faith in the Father

Several years ago a good friend of mine died. Her name was Rose Totino. Rose and her husband had started a frozen pizza business that was very successful. After Rose's husband died, she sold her business to a company that made her a vice president. But more important than her human achievements, Rose was a tremendous godly and holy woman.

When Rose was dying, her three daughters and her sons-in-law were all present by her side in the hospital room. Suddenly she cried out, "It's so bright. It's so bright!"

Her children began to question her, trying to figure out what she was seeing. She started to describe a rather marvelous scene, so one of her daughters asked, "Mama, is Jesus there?"

"Yes," she replied.

"Is he holding you?" she asked.

"Well, no. *I haven't died yet!* He's reaching for me. I can almost touch him."

Then Rose lapsed into unconsciousness. When she became conscious again, she began to utter, "It's so bright, you can't imagine it. It's like nothing you've seen." She quoted St. Paul's words in 1 Corinthians 2:9: "What no eye has seen, nor ear heard, nor the heart of man conceived, what God has prepared for those who love him."

As word traveled down the corridors that Rose was quickly approaching death, some of the doctors and nurses who were on duty came to her room. They came out of curiosity, because they had seen very few people die amid such an aura of peace. People were literally kneeling in her hospital room while Rose preached to them. She repeated over and over, "It's so bright, you can't imagine it. It's like nothing you've seen." Then she quoted St. Paul once again: "What no eye has seen, nor ear heard, nor the heart of man conceived, what God has prepared for those who love him."

Just after Rose had finished quoting this passage, she sat up, looked at everyone, and said, "The next one up, bring my sunglasses." Then she died. What a holy, delightful, and peaceful way to die! What faith!

God wants to give us this faith, "the assurance of things hoped for, the conviction of things not seen" (Heb 11:1). He wants to give us the assurance that we have a Father who loves us. He wants to give us the faith that we have a Lord, Master, and Savior who so loves us and so loves the Father that he gave everything for us. "And this is the confidence which we have in him, that if we ask anything according to his will he hears us" (1 Jn 5:14).

The abundant life can be ours, even now. But it will be life that is based on our relationship to our Father, based on the sure and firm hope of eternal life. The natural blessings of this life, good as they can be, will perish. But with God, abundance is ours.

CHAPTER 3

THE CHARACTERISTICS OF AN INTERCESSOR

He saw that there was no man, and wondered that there was no one to intervene.

ISAIAH 59:16

"I sought for a man among them who should build up the wall and stand in the breach before me for the land, that I should not destroy it; but I found none."

EZEKIEL 22:30

*I*n these passages God is speaking through two different prophets at two different times in history. But the essence of his message is the same: "I look around upon the face of the earth and I see injustice. I see the poor and oppressed. I see my people suffering. But there is no one to intervene." These are two of the most poignant moments in Scripture: The Lord is looking for intercessors to invoke his mercy on his people, yet he finds no one to intercede.

Most obviously, intercession is prayer for others. We take our concern for other people directly to God, asking his help on their behalf. St. Paul urges us always to pray for one another: "Pray at all times in the Spirit, with all prayer and supplication. To that end keep alert with all perseverance, making supplication for all the saints" (Eph 6:18).

When we speak of intercession as a ministry, however, we generally mean something broader than just saying a prayer for someone else. An intercessor makes a long-term decision to plead with God on behalf of another person or group of people. As intercessors, we literally "go between" the Lord and those we are praying for, asking him to show them his mercy and blessing. Ezekiel uses the image of a person "standing in the breach" between God and others to appeal for God's compassion and so avert his judgment.

We who are part of the new covenant know that it is Jesus Christ himself who is the one true intercessor for all humanity. Jesus was the one man who could bridge the gap. He was the one who could stand between heaven and earth, between God and man. It is Jesus Christ, the beloved Son of the Father, who stepped forward and said, "My food is to do the will of him who sent me, and to accomplish his work" (Jn 4:34). It is that same Jesus Christ who "always lives to make intercession for them" (Heb 7:25). At this precise moment, Jesus is praying for us. He is praying that the word of faith that we have heard again and again will take root in our hearts: faith to trust God on a deeper level and to surrender ourselves completely to God.

But Jesus invites us to become intercessors with him, to enter into his ministry of mercy and compassion for the world. The call to intercession is not just a duty for us as Christians but a privileged opportunity to share in the Lord's own work. In order to respond to this call, we need to strive to fashion our lives on God's Word to us in sacred Scripture. What, then, are some of the characteristics of an intercessor?

Righteousness

When we consider the increase of sin and rebellion in our own society, even among God's people, there is no question that today again we need intercessors to stand in the gap before God's judgment. Yet, "standing in the breach" means something more than only praying in intercession. It also refers to our personal righteousness. God will search a people for evidence of repentance, change, and righteousness. As we read in James 5:16: "The prayer of a righteous man has great power in its effects." To stand as intercessors between God's judgment and the sins of God's people, we must ourselves be living in freedom from serious sin. Our intercessory prayer should always include time for examination of our own conscience and repentance for our sins.

"Yes, but I keep on falling; I keep on sinning," you might say. That is entirely correct. You do. And so do I. Fortunately, we do not depend on our own efforts to achieve the righteousness that enables us to stand in the gap before God. Our righteousness comes through our faith in Jesus Christ. Righteousness means that we try to live by the law of God in the power of his Holy Spirit, and when we fail, we repent. As long as we follow this principle consistently, God hears our prayer.

We must never cease to pray. Rather, we should repeatedly repent of our sin and keep on praying. As we turn to Jesus with true conversion, true repentance, and true faith, he works in us to help us overcome sin and grow in holiness of life.

In an airport recently I noticed the many security badges and keys that the flight attendant at the gate was wearing around her neck. Particularly intriguing for me was a tag with the letters WWJD emblazoned on it—shorthand for "What Would Jesus Do?" Since we were still waiting to board, I decided to strike up a conversation with the attendant.

"Do you pay much attention to that?" I asked her, pointing to the tag.

"I actually do," she laughed. "It's a reminder to me when I'm dealing with people—especially irate, angry, frustrated, sick, and hurt people. I just keep saying it to myself."

I was impressed with her honesty and sincerity. We need to ask ourselves in every situation, "What would Jesus do?" And when we fail to do what Jesus would do, we need to take responsibility for our failure and repent. Then we have to have confidence that God will hear our prayer.

Did you ever begin to pray for a situation only to notice that it grew worse? Did you ever start to pray for someone and see things go downhill for that person? What was your response? Perhaps your response was to say, "My prayer is not effective." Or, "I'm too sinful," or, "God isn't listening to me." Ultimately your response might be, "I better stop praying."

But these are not the proper responses of a righteous person. Check first that you have repented for your sin. Then learn this truth! Often, the reason things get worse is because we have engaged the enemy, and we are exposing his guile. Through prayer, we have initiated a full-scale attack on the work of the devil. This is the reason why things get worse. And this is the *worst* time to stop praying!

Reliance on God and His Word

For many years I have been encouraging hundreds of thousands of people at conferences around the world that God's Word is living and true. I have told them that this Word is sharper than any two-edged sword and has the power to transform a person's life. The more you read it, ponder it, and live by it, I said, the more it will change you by God's grace.

Then I had the marvelous privilege to go to Lithuania. For the first time in many, many years, the country was free from the yoke of communism, which had left so many people in a spiritual vacuum. I thought I had faith. But when I arrived there, I discovered a people who have lived for years and years under oppression and domination. Their heads were bowed, and their bodies were bowed. I gave my first talk. Their heads were bowed at the beginning of my talk, and their heads were bowed at the end of my talk.

I turned to the Lord: "God, I don't know how to do this. I don't know how to reach your people. I don't know what to say. I don't know what to do. O God, maybe I was just the catalyst to get everybody else here. The other people who are with me are going to preach your word. Maybe I should just retire now and I'll pray for everybody else."

Two days later I was slated to give the second major talk at the second big rally. I awoke early that morning, got down on my knees, and said, "God, I don't know what to do. Please help me!" Since we were working through translators, the task before me was more complicated than I had thought it would be. Often my examples did not exactly translate into Lithuanian, and often my stories did not exactly translate either. In such a situation, one's personality, natural gifts, and even spiritual gifts do not exactly translate at times.

I cried out to God: "O God, if I just get up and read John 3:16 about your love for us, are you going to come? Are you there? Or if I just read Romans 5:6-8 about your love for us, will you come? Will you act?" I literally was scared. Why? Because I did not want to be humiliated. Once I repented of my pride, God began to touch my own heart with his love for his people.

At the rally I got up and started to speak those words from Scripture. "For God so loved the world that he gave his only Son, that whoever believes in him should not perish but have eternal life" (Jn 3:16). I told them that they were not abandoned. I told them that they were not orphans. "But God shows his love for us in that while we were yet sinners Christ died for us" (Rom 5:8).

When I began to speak, heads were bowed. But as I proclaimed these words from Scripture, I saw heads start to rise and eyes start to open. Then I began to see hands go up, and tears start to run down people's faces. I could only marvel: "O my God, you really are alive!"

Powerful Prayer

Of course, I know that God is alive, that he is here with us, and that he hears our prayer. But in that set of circumstances I was stripped of the things that I did not even know I was depending on. I was relying on so many things besides the Lord himself, the power of his Word, and the work of his Holy Spirit. When those things were suddenly taken away from me,

God revealed himself and his great love for that people.

God calls us to righteousness and holiness, not only so we can enjoy the fullness of eternal life but so that we can bring many other people to a saving knowledge of him. He will do it not by our strength but by our abandoning ourselves to his mercy, his power, and his Word: "Lord, I want to abide in you. I want to love you. I want to abandon myself to you. I want to surrender to you. I want to give my life to you. Come, Holy Spirit." This is the righteousness that James speaks about in his epistle. When we live out such righteousness in our lives, our prayer is powerful in its effects.

Occasionally a little knowledge of the meaning of a word in the original Greek or Hebrew can help us to better understand a particular passage from Scripture. This is one occasion when such knowledge is very revealing. Let me explain the word for power that James uses when he writes, "The prayer of a righteous man [or woman] has power in its effects." The Greek word that is usually used for power is *dounamis,* from which we get the English word *dynamite,* which means an explosion. But the word that is used in James 5:16 is *scruous,* which means "sustained explosion." It denotes an ongoing power. If we live righteously by putting our faith in God, trusting in his Word, relying on him, giving up the other things that we depend on, and casting ourselves on him, our prayer will have that sustained kind of power. Furthermore, this power does not depend on us; it depends on God.

A Repentant Spirit

I have already pointed out in chapter 1 the importance of the sacrament of confession in obtaining God's mercy for ourselves and sharing that mercy with others. Yet one of the elements of intercession that I find to be most important and often least discussed is the area of repentance for our sins. We can read about intercession, have the best gift of discernment, spend hours in prayer, make great sacrifices, and fast regularly, but even with all that our prayers can end up having no effect. In fact, our words can be like babble before the throne of God *if our hearts are not cleansed:* "For thou hast no delight in sacrifice; were I to give a burnt offering thou wouldst not be pleased. The sacrifice acceptable to God is a broken spirit; a broken and contrite heart, O God, thou wilt not despise" (Ps 51:16-17).

There are a number of sins in our lives that we can easily identify, acknowledge as wrongdoing, and take responsibility for. We need to bring those sins regularly to the throne of God and ask him for forgiveness. We need to be vigilant, so that we never fall into the habit of tolerating those sins by saying, "Yes, but that's just me. I'll never change." Such an attitude evinces hopelessness in that area—and a surrender to the spiral of sin.

Of course, it is true that we will have areas of weakness as long as we live. This is why we need a Savior *daily*. But to say that God does not want to help me or that God does not care about my sin, my weakness, is a lie and an indication of a lack of faith.

There can also be sins for which we fail to take responsibility. We rationalize our failures: "I wouldn't have done it if she hadn't said that." Or, "I wouldn't have acted that way if I didn't have that headache." But such extenuating circumstances do not matter. Our response should be to come before the Lord and say, "Lord, I'm sorry I did that. I'm responsible. Please forgive me."

We need to examine ourselves and see if we are avoiding responsibility for our sins. Often there are certain people or certain situations that make us prone to sinful patterns of speech or behavior. It is so easy in those circumstances to try to excuse ourselves. However, a mature Christian acknowledges his sin quickly and does not place the blame on others.

Even if you have good grounds to believe that the guilt is shared with another person, let God judge that person, and let that person's conscience do its part. Simply acknowledge what you did wrong. In other words, take clear ownership for your part and ask forgiveness. It is amazing how such a contrite spirit clears the air.

Finally, there might be hidden sins in our lives. Often we cannot look at these sins deep inside us, either because they cause us too much shame or because we have denied their existence so long that we do not "remember." God wants us to ask his Holy Spirit to help us bring that sin to mind or to have the courage to face it: "Behold, thou desirest truth in the inward being; therefore teach me wisdom in my secret heart" (Ps 51:6). God does not want to condemn us for these hidden sins; neither does he want us to spend our energy hiding or in fear of being discovered. He wants to bring his light of truth and mercy to bear on our weakness, so we can walk upright, clear and free before him as his sons and daughters.

The author of Psalm 51 goes on to pray: "Restore to me the joy of thy salvation, and uphold me with a willing spirit"

(Ps 51:12). This is the fruit of true and complete repentance. When we embrace it, we are in a better position to minister to others: "Then I will teach transgressors thy ways, and sinners will return to thee" (Ps 51:13).

One of the ways in which we can minister to others is through intercession. When our hearts are clean before the Lord (and this process, as we know, is not a one-time deal!), then we are most able to hear the Spirit teach us how to pray according to the mind of God—that is, in Jesus' name. We can experience the truth of the Lord's promise: "Whatever you ask in my name, I will do it, that the Father may be glorified in the Son" (Jn 14:13).

An Eternal Perspective

Over the years I have grown to appreciate how important it is for those of us who are engaged in a ministry of intercession to hold before ourselves the eternal perspective. This is especially true as we pray for our earthly needs.

The Lord certainly wants us to pray for our needs. Yet, as we pray, we must take care to insure that the intent or the purpose of our prayer is not limited to our earthly needs. Jesus tells us in Matthew 6:33, "Seek first his kingdom and his righteousness, and all these things shall be yours as well." We need to keep this "vision of heaven" in mind when we pray for ourselves and for others.

Daniel's Vision

I have found the readings for the Mass of the Feast of the Transfiguration helpful in understanding this eternal perspective. The first reading, from Daniel 7:9-10, 13-14 (NAB), presents a picture of what awaits us in heaven:

"As I watched: Thrones were set up and the Ancient One took his throne. His clothing was snow bright, and the hair on his head as white as wool; his throne was flames of fire, with wheels of burning fire. A surging stream of fire flowed out from where he sat; thousands upon thousands were ministering to him, and myriads upon myriads attended him. The court was convened and the books were opened.... As the visions during the night continued, I saw one like a son of man coming, on the clouds of heaven; when he reached the Ancient One and was presented before him, the one like a son of man received dominion, glory, and kingship; all peoples, nations, and languages serve him. His dominion is an everlasting dominion that shall not be taken away, his kingship shall not be destroyed."

What an awesome picture this is! The responsorial psalm follows with a call for us to have an eternal perspective, to acknowledge the Lord's sovereignty, and to be willing to follow him: "The Lord is king, the most high over all the earth."

Jesus Revealed

The Gospel reading is from Mark 9:2-10 (NAB). Jesus takes Peter, James, and John up to a high mountain, where he is transfigured before them. Furthermore, Moses and Elijah appear with Jesus and converse with him. Then the voice of the Father cries out from the heavens: "This is my beloved Son. Listen to him." Needless to say, Peter, James, and John are terrified.

In a certain way, the disciples were without a clue up to this point. They had no idea what the resurrection from the dead meant; they had never seen a resurrection. And they had no idea what the supernatural, eternal effects of Jesus' resurrection would mean. Yet, look what Jesus does for his disciples! He knew what lay ahead, including his suffering and death and their betrayal, denial, and fear. He knew of the disciples' own persecution and martyrdom. He wanted to give them a vision of who God was, a vision of heaven, that would sustain them in the very difficult times to come.

We need to ask God to give us such a moment of transfiguration when we recognize Jesus for who he truly is. The grace of this moment will sustain us, as well as those for whom we are praying, through trials and difficulties.

Our Eyes Fixed on Him

We go back to the second reading for the Feast of the Transfiguration. There St. Peter comments on his own experience of Jesus' transfiguration, now that he understands even more clearly how important that revelation of Jesus was and how important it is to *listen* to Jesus: "We ourselves heard this voice come from heaven while we were with him on the holy mountain. Moreover, we possess the prophetic message that is altogether reliable. You will do well to be attentive to it, as to a lamp shining in a dark place, until day dawns and morning star rises in your hearts" (2 Pt 1:18-19, NAB).

Peter is reminding us to cling to this message. This eternal perspective will be like a lamp shining in the darkness for us until the day of eternity dawns. It is very easy to focus on the bad things that are happening and to feel that our prayers are not being heard. But if we keep our eyes fixed on Jesus and listen to him, he will sustain us as we pray.

How much of an eternal perspective do you have? Read stories about heaven. Read the lives of the saints, especially those who have had visions of heaven or revelations about heaven. You will discover that this eternal perspective sustained them when God demanded incredible sacrifices of them—things that would break the endurance of most of us.

Ask the Holy Spirit for an eternal perspective; it is a gift that he gives to everyone who asks for it. God is merciful. He did it for Peter, James, and John because he knew what they would eventually have to endure; he who knows all things, who knows every aspect of our lives, will hear our prayer, too, and answer it.

Then we can pray for others with a new hope and confidence—and with a new perspective of what is really important for each person.

CHAPTER 4

BECOMING A PERSON OF PRAYER

C learly, developing an intimate, personal relationship with God is perhaps the most important step of all toward becoming a true intercessor. Thus it is of utmost importance that an intercessor be a person of prayer. In fact, we as intercessors have to make a commitment to pray daily.

Why is it important to pray daily? Prayer is intangible in a certain way; we cannot always see its effects. If we do not pray daily, we lose contact with Jesus—the one we love. We lose contact with the only one who can give us wisdom, insight, and understanding so we can live in peace, joy, and confidence. We eventually fail in our strength.

Yet when we pray, our special needs and special people are sometimes very much on our minds. Consequently our prayer can become a list of requests rather than a time of worship, praise, and communion with God, where we sit before the Lord and ask for his insight, wisdom, and understanding so that we might follow him more closely.

Moses is a remarkable example of an intercessor who took time to develop a "face-to-face" relationship with God, a prayer relationship in which God became his intimate friend. The authors of the Old Testament were struck by the intimacy with which Moses could talk to God: "There has not arisen a prophet since in Israel like Moses, whom the Lord knew face to face" (Dt 34:10). Moses' face shone with light after his encounters with the Lord, so that no one else could bear to see his unveiled face (see Exodus 34:34-35).

We are offered the privilege of knowing God even more intimately than Moses. As we have already seen, we can come to God as his own children, in the name of his beloved Son Jesus, with the help and intercession of the Holy Spirit.

Time With the Lord

How do we develop a truly intimate relationship with God? As in everything, the real initiative comes from God. The Lord wants to be our friend; he wants to have a deeply personal relationship with us. Yet, as in any relationship, we must also take steps to open our hearts and our lives so that a true friendship can develop.

That means making sure we take time for prayer each day. In addition to examining our lives for sins and negative attitudes that could block our relationship with God, it means learning the truth about God through careful study of Scripture and the teaching of the Church. And it means allowing time in our prayer for silence, for listening to God, for waiting upon his action. It also means making a sincere attempt to incorporate the various forms of prayer that have come down to us through Scripture and the writings of the early Church Fathers: prayer of adoration; prayer of petition; prayer of thanksgiving; and prayer of praise.

Make it a point to regularly check your progress in daily

prayer. Are you taking time each day to read Scripture? Then do you ask the Lord how it applies to your life? Do you ask the Lord what he wants of you each day? Do you ask him how you are doing in *his* eyes? Do you read the psalms and worship the Lord each day?

There will be days when you are terribly distracted or upset. If this is the case, seek ways to overcome the distraction or the emotional turmoil that you are experiencing. For example, listen to a good Christian music tape. It will help lift your heart and your spirit to the Lord. Join in the singing. You will be amazed how quickly it will help you enter into worship and praise.

After you have taken some time to feed on God's Word and to worship him, adore him, and praise him, put your needs into his hands for the day. Then pray for the people and the situations that are on your mind.

Give Thanks

When we are praying for other people or for the state of the world in general, it is easy to focus on the negative: the problems, the needs, the seeming hopelessness. Perhaps that is why the apostle Paul always made a point of encouraging people both to intercede and to give thanks: "First of all, then, I urge that supplications, prayers, intercessions, and thanksgiving be made for all men" (1 Tm 2:1); "Have no anxiety about anything, but in everything by prayer and supplication with thanksgiving let your requests be made known to God" (Phil 4:6).

I think our intercessory prayers have much greater power when they are combined with thanksgiving for all that the Lord *has* done. For one thing, thanksgiving builds our faith, reminding us of all the ways that God has already shown his love for us and for those we are praying for.

Of course, it's hard to think of much reason to be thankful in certain situations. Things may be getting worse rather than better; we may feel that God has not heard or answered our prayers at all. Even at those times, however, we can give thanks to the Lord in faith that he is at work. In some cases, we can even be thankful that things are getting worse: sometimes a problem has to get worse before people become open to real change.

Above all, we can give thanks simply that we are able to bring our problems and concerns to the Lord. How privileged we are to approach God as our loving Father, in the name of his Son Jesus, through the power of the Holy Spirit!

Supplement your daily prayer time with some good spiritual reading. Biographies of the saints can be a source of tremendous inspiration and encouragement for each and every one of us. There are also a myriad of good, solid Christian books to help us grow in our understanding of almost every aspect of the Christian life. Let such books be a source of inspiration, wisdom, and challenge. Just don't let a book be an escape from personal, intimate time with God. Nothing can replace that!

Praying Constantly

When you have mastered some of the basic elements of prayer and incorporated them into your daily life, think about ways in which you can envelop your entire day in prayer. In 1 Thessalonians 5:17 St. Paul urges us to pray "constantly," "unceasingly," or "at every opportunity" (depending on what translation of Scripture you are reading).

The thought of praying constantly may seem overwhelming. After all, most people find it hard enough to pray for half an hour each day; nevertheless, a regular prayer time is essential. However, for someone with a very busy schedule, praying constantly may really prove easier than getting a fixed prayer time. All it really takes is attention, so that you remember to pray throughout the day, and perhaps some creativity at blending your prayer with other activities. You need to follow the guidance of the Holy Spirit on when and how to pray for your regular intentions. Often it is not possible to squeeze them all in on a particular day.

I once received a letter from a young woman who told me how the Lord had taught her to "pray unceasingly" at her summer job in an ice cream parlor.

"Other summers I have tried to pray while working," she explained, "but it never lasted long. I would say an Our Father or Hail Mary while putting a customer's order together. Then I'd have to stop and try to remember if they had wanted a small or medium shake, chocolate or vanilla, etc. The problem was that praying had nothing to do with what I was doing.

"So last summer the Lord began to show me how he would have me pray at work. As I squirted flavoring into a shake, I would pray, 'Let your grace fall down on this customer. Let him taste your goodness.' Or when I crowned a sundae with whipped cream, I'd ask the Lord to award the customer the crown of life."

She went on to say that her new method of prayer completely changed her attitude toward her work. "Whereas before I had dreaded going into that hot, sticky little place, I came to enjoy working there. The Lord gave me some type of prayer for virtually everything that I had to do. So I was in non-stop prayer for however long my shift was."

Praying constantly *is* possible. Whether it means stopping at your desk for just a minute every hour or so for a few words of intercession, or praying while you fold laundry or cook, there are moments you can turn into intercession for those you love.

Perseverance

Perseverance (or persistence) in prayer is a hallmark of any true intercessor. Jesus taught us its value when he told the parable of the persistent widow and the judge (see Lk 18:1-8). In fact, St. Luke prefaces his account of the parable with the moral: "And he told them a parable, to the effect that they ought always to pray and not lose heart" (Lk 18:1).

It appears that a judge, who "neither feared God nor cared about men," was constantly being pestered by a certain widow. We do not know the exact nature of her complaint; Jesus simply says that she kept pleading for her rights. Perhaps she merely wanted bread for her children. In any case, the judge refused to deal with her complaint for a long time. Yet the widow persisted. She must have been banging day after day on his door, because the judge finally decided that he was prepared to do anything to shut her up: "Though I neither fear God nor regard man, yet because this widow bothers me, I will vindicate her, or she will wear me out by her continual coming" (Lk 18:4-5).

Then Jesus tells us: "Hear what the unrighteous judge says. And will not God vindicate his elect, who cry to him day and night? Will he delay long over them? I tell you, he will vindicate them speedily. Nevertheless, when the Son of man comes, will he find faith on earth?" (Lk 18:6-8).

Jesus clearly encourages persistence in prayer. He encourages us to bang on the door and to continue banging whether it takes three, five, or fifteen years! At the same time, we need to recognize our human limitations and admit that we cannot see the whole picture. We have to ask the Holy Spirit to guide us in our prayer. If our prayer does not correspond to what the Lord wants, we need to ask the Holy Spirit to show us how we can adjust our prayer so that we are always praying in Jesus' name.

A Testimony to Perseverance

Back in 1986, I spoke at a large conference in New England about the wonderful practice of setting aside the first Friday of every month for prayer and fasting. I encouraged those present to intercede in this way for their special intentions. I also asked them to share with me any blessings they eventually received that they felt they could attribute to this prayer.

A few years ago I received a letter from a woman who was at that conference. Hers is a wonderful testimony of persistence in prayer. She wrote:

"It has taken me eleven years to answer your request to write to you if any blessing is given to us who have prayed and fasted on the first Friday of the month, starting in September of 1986. I have three daughters. My third is Lisa. She started on drugs at age thirteen. Her father walked out on the family the following year, after we started to pray and fast. Then she started running away, moved into hard drugs, prostitution, abortion, prison, and finally contracted AIDS. I think I was the only mother in the whole United States who was happy when her daughter was in prison. There she was safe, got three meals a day, became clean. I could send her religious books and a rosary.

"My two oldest daughters went on to college, married nice men after school, and have large families. But for Lisa, there was only pain and suffering. Yet, I continued to pray.

"In 1992 Lisa moved into an AIDS residence that was set up by the archdiocese of Boston—one of the first AIDS residences in this country. There she came back to the Church and started lectoring at daily Mass. She even had all the black Baptists there saying the rosary! She died in the Lord on June 21, 1993. Incidentally, she always wanted to go to Medjugorje, so it has to be a God-incidence that her wake and funeral were held on June 24 and 25, the anniversary of the apparitions there.

"But there's more. We continued to pray and fast daily. My second daughter was married in the Catholic Church to a wonderful man, who, unfortunately, was very anti-Catholic.

They continued going to an Episcopal church after their wedding and after four children and many rosaries, her husband finally entered the Catholic Church this Easter. We had five first communions this year!

"My son-in-law sort of came crashing in. He's read all of the Pope's encyclicals. He's given his testimony on our local Catholic cable TV station. He's gone on a retreat with John Michael Talbot. On top of that, he's taken my grandchildren out of public school and is sending them to parochial school. Can you believe it?

"There's even more," she wrote in closing, "but this gives you a picture of how powerful the moment is that you started at the conference in 1986."

Of course, I did not start that moment. God did. Persevere in prayer!

Aware of the Enemy

Keep in mind that the devil loves to tell you by every means possible that your prayer is ineffective. He wants you to believe that your prayer does not matter and that God does not hear you. Needless to say, this is an outright lie!

Always be vigilant and ready to expose the devil. Do not allow him to rob you of faith or of the powerful weapon of prayer. Tell him to go to hell! He is the one person you can say that to in good conscience—and as often as you want!

Years ago, John Wesley said, "Give me a hundred men who hate nothing but sin, who fear nothing but God, and who know nothing but Jesus Christ and him crucified, and I will shake the world." Together with our Lord Jesus Christ, we have the power to make a difference in the world. We can thwart the enemy if we focus on God, *his* power, *his* work, and *his* plan.

CHAPTER 5

WE ARE THE BRANCHES

I am the true vine, and my Father is the vinedresser. Every branch of mine that bears no fruit, he takes away, and every branch that does bear fruit he prunes, that it may bear more fruit. You are already made clean by the word which I have spoken to you. Abide in me, and I in you. As the branch cannot bear fruit by itself, unless it abides in the vine, neither can you, unless you abide in me. I am the vine, you are the branches. He who abides in me, and I in him, he it is that bears much fruit, for apart from me you can do nothing. If a man does not abide in me, he is cast forth as a branch and withers; and the branches are gathered, thrown into the fire and burned. If you abide in me, and my words abide in you, ask whatever you will, and it shall be done for you. By this my Father is glorified, that you bear much fruit, and so prove to be my disciples. As the Father has loved me, so have I loved you; abide in love.

JOHN 15:1-9

When I traveled to Israel for the first time, I was somewhat amazed that the grapevines there were very different from the small ones that used to grow in my grandparents' backyard in Pennsylvania. In Israel the grapevines actually look like trees. The trunks are quite large in diameter, with branches growing out of them. This observation gave me a new perspective on this very familiar passage from Scripture.

When I used to read this passage, I would envision the small, bush-sized grapevines that I had known in my childhood. (Even so, they managed to produce a good number of grapes each year.) I always thought this passage was merely a commentary on Christian unity. We Christians, I thought, were all part of some massive network of a vine. If you traced the branches back, you would find that they were all rooted in the central branch, which was Christ. I failed to grasp the strength and the power that Jesus wished to convey to us in this passage.

Then I saw for myself the grapevines with which Jesus was familiar. When he tells us, "I am the vine; you are the branches," he is reminding us that he is the stock—a large, solid trunk from which we grow. Life flows to us from him. He is the source of nourishment, and he is the source of power. His life flowing though us enables us to produce fruit. Jesus ardently desires to give us his life.

Life From the Vine

How do we receive his life? How do we bear fruit? First of all, we have to put our faith in the *person* of Jesus Christ, rather than in what he does for us. We need to recognize that *he is who he says he is* and that *he is true to his promises;* we need to begin to live out of that reality.

On a visit to Lithuania I was talking to a group about the challenges they had faced as Catholics before the collapse of the communist regime. They told me the story of a group of people who were caught coming out of church one night at a time when people were prohibited from attending church services. A group of soldiers confronted them: "All we ask you to do is to spit on this crucifix. Nothing else. Deny your faith."

Most of the people in the group reacted by saying, "I've got family. I have responsibilities. God knows in my heart that I am not denying him. So, as long as I think this way, I can do this external act." I certainly can understand the dilemma they were facing, and I can understand how their emotions could easily cloud their reasoning. Among them was a sixteen-year-old girl, though, who was stalwart in her faith. "I cannot deny him," she retorted. Then she took the crucifix and kissed it. The soldiers shot her right there. Do we have this same kind of faith?

This young girl was in love with the person of Jesus Christ. For her, faith was not primarily a set of doctrines to which she had to adhere. Faith did not consist of ceremonies that she had to attend. Faith was not a series of things she had to do. This young girl knew the very person of Jesus Christ, and this was her source of faith.

When God says, "I am the vine; you are the branches," he is telling us that he wants to impart to us the same grace that he gave that sixteen-year-old girl. He wants us to receive life from him.

Rooted in the Father

After seeing the grapevines in Israel, I learned about another very famous grapevine growing in London, England, at a place called Hampton Court. This vine has been bearing fruit since the late 1800s. It is famous not only for its longevity but also for its fruitfulness. It produces over two thousand clusters of grapes in a single season. (A "normal" vine produces between thirty and eighty clusters in a season.)

Needless to say, viticulturists are fascinated with this grapevine, and it has been the subject of countless studies. One study focused on its extensive root system. Scientists discovered that the roots followed a very complex and circuitous trajectory until they found their way into the River Thames. Further studies revealed that the rich muck of the river furnished countless nutrients to the grapevine. The scientists were even more amazed when they realized that these nutrients had to travel almost two miles from the River Thames in order to provide nourishment to the vine. The life that is coming up from the river is being turned into a rich sap that is feeding the branches of that grapevine.

I have a framed picture of this famous grapevine in my office, courtesy of some friends who took pictures of it when they were there. The Lord has used that vine to teach me some important spiritual truths about fostering faith. First of all, faith is not something that we can take for granted, and it is not something that we receive only once. Faith is an ongoing process. We have to take active and concrete steps to foster it.

At that time I felt that the Lord was telling me: "I didn't just go two miles for you; I went to my death so that you could receive life. I'm rooted in the Father. I want to nourish you with that life. I want you to receive that kind of life, so that you can bear abundant fruit."

When I reread Jesus' words in John 15:1-9, I noticed that Jesus makes several references to the fact that the branches of the grapevine will bear more and more fruit. Furthermore, he progressively quantifies the amount of fruit. First he alludes to the fact that the branches of the vine "bear fruit." Then he tells us that God will trim those branches so that they will be "even more fruitful." Finally, he assures us that if we remain in him and he remains in us, we will "bear much fruit."

Since then, I have made it a practice to do two things each day. First, I say at least once a day, "Thank you, God, for the faith you have given me." And secondly, each day I pray, "Please give me more faith, God." I do this because I have realized that faith is a gift. I know that I need to ask God for the gift of faith and, if I do so, he will give it to me.

If you want your faith to grow to the point where you know beyond a shadow of a doubt that Jesus Christ is your Lord and Savior and that he lives within you—a truly living, vibrant faith—you only have to ask him. He will give you that kind of faith. He will help your faith grow beyond your obligation to attend Sunday Mass, obey the Ten Commandments, and follow the precepts of the Church.

If you already have a personal relationship with the Lord, do not hesitate to ask him to increase your faith each and every day. There is always room for growth. Faith is a gift that God freely gives us. The spark of that gift is given to us in baptism and fanned into a flame at confirmation. But if we do not know we have it or if we ignore it, we are not going to use it and it dies down by disuse. But if we thank the Lord each day for the faith he has given us and ask him to give us more, he *will* increase our faith.

The Way of Obedience

The second way to foster faith is by being obedient to the Lord—by following through on what the Lord calls you to do. When you are in love with a person, you want to do what that person wants.

Many years ago some friends who were attending a charismatic conference at the University of Notre Dame met together during lunch for a time of prayer. Among them was an eight-year-old boy. He was there with his uncle, who was a priest. As the group was praying, this little boy turned to his uncle and said, "Uncle Frank, I think God wants to say something." Everyone's ears perked up. There is always something special about little children, especially when they intervene in adult situations. Because of their innocence and purity, we feel as if we touch the life of God when we are near them. Everyone looked at the boy. Someone asked, "What does God want to say?"

His words were so simple, yet so profound: "Well, God says, 'I am God and you are not God. I tell you what to do. You do not tell me what to do. If I tell you to climb a tree, climb a tree. If I tell you to dig a hole, dig a hole.' That's all."

Those who were present were not only touched; they were astonished by the simple lesson that the Lord was teaching them through the mouth of this eight-year-old boy. And so was I when I heard this story. Since that time, I have referred to it on numerous occasions to illustrate the need to simply obey what God asks of us and to conform our will to his will.

But the story does not end there. A few years ago I received a letter from this now young man. He wrote: "I hear that you have been telling the story of the word that the Lord gave me years ago. I am in my mid-twenties now, and that word shaped my life."

God is perfectly good. He wants the very best for us, and we can trust him. Nonetheless, God is not safe in the sense that we can conform him to what *we* want. God does not come to do our bidding; we come to do his. If we are going to let God lead us into the fullness of life, we have to conform our will to his will.

Sometimes this call to obedience can take some interesting turns. I had such an experience several years ago when I was studying the Gospel of John. I was reading John 13:34, where Jesus says, "A new commandment I give to you, that you love one another; even as I have loved you, that you also love one another." I said to myself, "This is a difficult word. This is real tough." At the same time, I felt the Lord was saying to me in the back of my mind, "Eat my word."

My immediate reaction was to reiterate my desire to fully obey God's word to me: "Oh, yes, Lord, I want to obey you. I want your Word to shape my life. Yes, Lord. I want to chew on your Word. I want your Word to be part of me."

Yet the same thought kept coming to me and would not go away: "Eat my word."

"What do you mean, Lord?" I asked again. Once again the same thought came back: "Eat my word."

Finally I decided that the Lord wanted me to take his word literally. I took my Bible and a pair of scissors, and I carefully cut out the words "Love one another as I have loved you." I put the little piece of paper in my mouth, chewed it, and swallowed it. It was a symbolic act that I felt the Lord was calling me to do, as a way of expressing my desire to obey him and be one with his word. Amazingly, I have to admit that something happened in me through that symbolic gesture. Something opened up in me, and I felt the sap of the Holy Spirit, the life of God, flowing more in me.

When Mother Teresa left her religious order, the Sisters of Loreto, in the 1940s, she was only taking the next step God had for her in her life. She had no idea at the time that she would make an impact on the entire world. She had no idea that the work she initiated at that time would take off like it did. She was simply obeying God's word to her at that moment in her life. If we are obedient to the little things that God asks of us, he will multiply them and fan them into a flame. God blesses his servants for their obedience to him.

Infinite Love

Whenever you read or hear Jesus' words, "I am the vine; you are the branches," think of that vine in Hampton Court. Think of the life that Jesus wants to give you. Remember that Jesus loves you so much he died for you. If you had been the only person on the face of this earth, God would have died for you. He loves you that much.

No one can say, "I am totally unloved, abandoned, and rejected." There is no truth to these words. Yet Satan loves to entertain us with such thoughts in an effort to rob us of God's truth.

Several years ago the religious community to which I belong, the Servants of God's Love, took on a new apostolate.

We started to provide foster care for medically fragile children. Since then we have cared for many children for varying lengths of time. However, the first baby for whom we cared will always be very special to us. We took care of her for almost three years before she was adopted. When she was entrusted to our care, she only weighed three and a half pounds. I literally could hold her in my hand. Her little body had a gray-blue color to it, and she shook from the effects of the drug addiction that she had inherited from her birth mother.

On the third night after she came to us, I had her in my arms and was rocking her, trying to feed her with a doll bottle since she was too small to drink from a normal bottle. In fact, if you put a pacifier in her mouth, the top of the pacifier would hit her forehead. As I was feeding her, the Lord very clearly said to me, "I would die for her. I love her infinitely."

We human beings get so caught up with size, quantity, and material value. But God knows the infinite value of a soul. God loves each individual person, and he cares for each individual person. Jesus reassures each one of us, "As the Father has loved me, so have I loved you."

Pruning

While I was in Israel I asked a man who was caring for the grapevines to give me a little lesson on pruning. I suspected that even a short explanation would enhance my understanding of Scripture, and I certainly was not disappointed.

"Right after the harvest," he said, "after the vine has borne fruit, it is cut back. The branches are cut back to within one to two inches of the stock. For the following nine months, all the nourishment goes into the stock so that it gets bigger, and so that it can hold not only the weight of the new branches, but also the weight of even more fruit."

Have you ever done something that seemed to be spiritually fruitful, only to experience everything going wrong afterwards? Have you ever been disappointed because you did something that seemed so right spiritually but produced little or no fruit? How many times have you conceived of some wonderful plan, yet you never got around to doing it for one reason or another? Nonetheless, it is often at such times that the life of Christ is growing within us. How should we respond? We should just sit back and let it happen!

Several years ago I experienced a period of intense spiritual dryness that lasted for over four years. During that time every venture I undertook to serve the Lord seemed to bear meager fruit or no fruit at all. During that period the Lord kept saying to me, "You decrease; I increase." In retrospect I realized that the life of Christ was growing within me. When I was finally able to yield myself to the work of his Holy Spirit, I began to experience uncounted blessings.

A Continual Process

Going back to my little lesson in pruning grapes, the man elaborated: "For about nine months, nothing happens in the branches. They are just these pruned, cut-down, cut-off nubs of branches. But the stock grows bigger. Then, within a month or two, the branches suddenly begin to sprout, and they grow bigger and richer than before. If it is a good, healthy stock, it bears more fruit than the year before. Then the grapevine is cut back again."

Jesus knew all this when he was talking about the vine and the branches. The people who were listening to him were also familiar with the pruning process and understood what he was saying. They knew that God did not prune them just once in their life. They knew that the pruning process would be repeated over and over again.

I learned still more about the pruning process from my guide. "Do you know that grapevines need constant pruning?" he asked me. "The big pruning happens once a year. But a good vinedresser will go out every day and examine all his grapevines. You see, they get these little feeders that come out. We call them bones because they get very hard. Vinedressers constantly have to cut them off because they can wrap themselves around the vine and choke some of the branches. So the vinedresser is always out and cutting. Another thing: grapevines love to turn in on themselves instead of facing the sun. They constantly have to be pruned and turned to face the sun."

By this point I was thoroughly fascinated. Grapevines are so much like us! When we are left unchecked, we have that very same tendency to turn in on ourselves. Because of our sinful nature, we naturally tend to focus on ourselves and turn away from God, the very source of life!

The Process

How does God prune us? He undoubtedly has many ways, but the three that I have experienced in my own life are through sin, weakness, and misfortune.

Sin. Even though I sincerely wish I did not sin, and in spite of my best efforts, I still manage to sin a lot. One of the key ways is by being very critical in my mind. Even though this type of sin is not visible to those around me, I am keenly aware of its presence in my life and I am constantly waging battle with it.

A number of years ago I took a leap in faith and prayed a very dangerous prayer: "Lord, whatever you need to do to change me, do it. I want my mind to be like your mind." He has answered my prayer every day since then, even though I have tried to rescind it on many occasions.

For example, I have noticed that whenever I criticize someone for something, I do exactly the same thing within twenty-four hours. As a result, I have been humiliated and embarrassed on many occasions.

The day after I prayed this prayer for the first time, I was traveling on a plane. A couple of rows in front of me I spotted a man who was holding a cup of hot coffee in his hand, talking and gesturing to the person next to him.

"Honest to goodness," I said to myself, "you'd think he'd be more careful. Men are thoughtless. Look at him, he's going to burn somebody."

At that moment a flight attendant walked by and bumped against him, and the coffee spilled all over her uniform. I sat back smugly. I had known it was going to happen!

At the time I did not drink coffee. But about twenty minutes later I had this sudden urge for a cup of coffee and asked the flight attendant to bring me one. Even though the outcome might seem so obvious, I never made the connection at that moment. The flight attendant gave me a cup of coffee, and immediately afterwards the man across the aisle from me began to engage me in a conversation.

My father always told me that I could not talk without using my hands. He used to say to me, "Just sit on your hands for a moment and see if you can explain it to me without using your hands." I never could.

So as this man and I were busily engaged in our conversation, another poor, unsuspecting flight attendant walked down the aisle and bumped against me, and the coffee spilled all over her uniform. It was as though I could hear the Lord saying loudly and clearly, "See!"

On another occasion I happened to be working side by side with a dear sister in the Lord. "She's so inefficient," I began to think. "I mean, really, if she just did this and this and this, we could get all this stuff done so much faster." I went the whole nine yards with that thought.

For the next three days I found that I could do nothing right. I was late for everything. I fell down the stairs trying to get somewhere. Nothing seemed to work. The message was clear: God was nailing my face to the ground. God was pruning me.

I also have an ongoing struggle with impatience. One morning I was driving to Mass at a church about six miles from my home, mainly down a country road. I was late, but the speed limit on that road is fifty miles an hour, so I thought I would be able to make up for the lost time. Suddenly I found myself behind a car that was going thirty-five miles per hour. To complicate matters, there was a double yellow line down the road, so there was little chance of passing it.

I was right up against the bumper of that car, venting my impatience. Finally I had an opportunity to pass it, so I pulled out. I took a quick glance to see who was driving. It was an older woman. I roared ahead, pulled up in front of the church, and ran in. As I dipped my finger into the holy water font, I realized that the congregation was just finishing the opening hymn. "Oh good, I got here in time," I said to myself. "O God, I'm so glad to be here to worship you." I knelt down in a pew.

Within three or four minutes the door opened. The woman who had been in the car in front of me came in and knelt down across the aisle from me. "Oh, no," I thought. "But she won't know who I am. It doesn't matter."

During Mass I heard the Lord saying, "Repent to her."

I tried dismissing the thought from my mind, but it kept coming back to me. Finally, when Mass was over, I went across the aisle.

"Pardon me," I whispered into her ear. She turned, looked at me, and said, "Aren't you Ann Shields from the TV show *The Choices We Face?*"

"Yes, I am. I would like to repent to you for being so impatient when I was behind you this morning in the car."

"I thought that was you!" she replied.

What embarrassment! What humiliation! Yet, it is through these little embarrassing, humiliating incidents that God prunes us. When God prunes you through your sin, thank him for it. When your sin is exposed, or when you see the effects of your sin, repent. God is pruning you so that the life of Christ can grow in you.

Weakness. God also prunes us through our weaknesses. We all have weaknesses. One of mine is that I want to please everybody. Unfortunately, it is impossible; any effort in this regard ends up being a dead-end street. Nevertheless, I tried to do it for many years.

When the Lord told me that I had to decrease so that he might increase, he began to work in this area of my life. During the following four years I found that I could not make anybody happy in spite of my best efforts to do so. Repeatedly the Lord told me to set aside my own agenda, my own plans, and my own ways to make people happy. I was to listen to him and to trust him.

Misfortune. God also prunes us through misfortune. When I was in Lithuania shortly after the fall of communism, a man in his seventies came up to me during one of the ministry sessions at the conference we were conducting and asked for prayer. My translator and prayer partner told him we would be glad to pray for him. We asked him what he would like us to pray for. He began to tell us about his life. His father and his brother had both been shot and killed. Another brother had starved to death in prison. He had seen something horrible happen to one of his sisters.

Any one of these things would have been a wrenching experience for someone, but all of them together seemed too much for one person to have to bear. We were sure that this man needed prayer so that he would be able to forgive and receive healing. So we asked him, "Would you like us to pray for healing and forgiveness?"

He looked up at us with a big smile and said, "Oh, no. I've forgiven. What I want to pray for is that my enemies will receive the same grace that I have, that they will know the life of Jesus Christ."

I was dumbfounded. In all humility, I could only say, "We'll pray with you. But then will you pray with us? There are a lot of things, much smaller, that we are holding on to, things that we haven't forgiven."

In spite of this man's terrible tragedy and misfortune, he was still able to accept God's pruning work in his life and bear abundant fruit. Like most people, he probably experienced bitterness, resentment, hatred, and a desire for revenge at various times. But he prayed for greater faith and for a special grace, and God gave it to him. God's light shone in the face of that man.

At that same conference I talked to two other men who had spent seventeen years in prison camps in Siberia before being released. For all those years they had to deal with freezing temperatures and backbreaking work. It was a mystery to me how they ever survived it. Unfortunately, they returned with nothing but bitterness and a desire for revenge in their hearts. I could only pray, "God, give them the grace to forgive." I knew that if they failed to do so, their bitterness would eventually destroy them.

God prunes us through sin. God prunes us through weakness. And God prunes us through misfortune. Ask him to show you what he is doing in your life. Ask him to help you receive the life that he wants to give you through his pruning action so that his life might grow in you.

Mother Teresa regularly prayed a little prayer that Cardinal John Newman composed: "Shine in me, and so be in me, that all with whom I come into contact may know thy presence in my soul. Let them look up and see no longer me but only Jesus." Frankly, the only thing worth living for is that those who see us might see Jesus. Pruning is one of the ways in which our life decreases and God's life increases.

CHAPTER 6

IN THE NAME OF JESUS

"Truly, truly, I say to you, he who believes in me will also do the works that I do; and greater works than these will he do, because I go to the Father. Whatever you ask in my name, I will do it, that the Father may be glorified in the Son; if you ask anything in my name, I will do it."

JOHN 14:12-14

Many times in the past I would read this passage and immediately try to apply it without fully understanding what Jesus meant. I would say, "Jesus, in your name, do this." Or, "Jesus, in your name, make this happen." Yet, is the name of Jesus just a formula we can attach to the end of any prayer request we make?

I realize now that I was rather naive in my understanding of what Jesus meant, but I take consolation in the fact that I was not alone. Indeed, many illustrious teachers often gave teachings along these same lines. What does it really mean to pray "in the name of Jesus"?

What Does God Want?

Consider what it usually means to make a request in someone else's name. If I were to ask you for money in the name of Mother Teresa of Calcutta, for example, you would rightly expect your money to help Mother Teresa's work. If I asked you to sign a petition in the name of the Right to Life movement, you would expect your signature to support the Right to Life movement. If it turned out I was actually taking your money or signature for my own purposes, you would be justifiably angry.

In the same way, if we are praying "in the name of Jesus," our requests should have some connection with Jesus and his work. In other words, I had better have some reason to think that I am asking for something Jesus wants! When we are sincerely praying "in the name of Jesus," we do not simply say the name of Jesus at the end of our prayer. We are praying according to Jesus' heart and Jesus' intention.

When you have been pruned and the life of Christ is increasing in your life, you love him so much that you find yourself saying, "I want whatever is your will." This is what it means to ask in the name of Jesus. The only way you can know whether something is according to Jesus' nature and according to Jesus' will is by union with him.

When I was a child there was a small grocery store on the corner near our house. My father owned a gas station nearby. If he was busy and we needed something at the house, he would send me to the store to buy it. "Tell them your dad sent you, and I'll take care of the bill," he instructed. So I would go into the store and say, "My dad told me to get a quart of milk and a loaf of bread." And they would give them to me.

I was asking in my father's name, and they trusted that what I was asking for was exactly what my father intended me to buy. If I had gone into the store and told them instead that my father wanted me to get ten candy bars, they probably would have questioned me to ascertain that it was indeed what my father wanted and not what I wanted! Since everyone respected my father and knew that I was trustworthy, I could confidently walk into the store and ask for something that I knew very well he wanted.

If you examine Holy Scripture closely and study the customs and traditions of those times, you will discover that people in biblical times would use a person's name in ordinary conversation only when they were intimately connected with that person in some way. For example, they would use a person's name when they had a close family connection with that person. The person was not simply an acquaintance; he or she was an intimate friend or relative. They knew that person's heart and mind, and they knew that person's will. When Jesus says, "If you ask anything in my name, I will do it," he is implying that we know his mind, will, and heart when we invoke his name—that we are truly his disciples.

How do we get to know Jesus in this way? How can we know his mind? How can we know his will? And how can we know his heart?

Living in Christ

First and foremost, we have to make our home in Christ and let his Word make its home in us. This is exactly what Jesus meant when he said, "If you abide in me, and my words abide in you, ask whatever you will, and it shall be done for you" (Jn 15:7). We need to read, study, and ponder God's Word to us in Scripture so that it takes root in us.

Many years ago, when I first began to experience the power of intercessory prayer, I was thoroughly excited by the power that Jesus makes available to us. My immediate response was to pray for every need and every intention that popped into my mind. Instead of seeking guidance from the Lord as to what I should pray for, I found *myself* deciding what to pray for.

One day as I sat down to pray for the many intentions that had accumulated on my list, I felt as though the Lord put his hand on my shoulder and said, "Wait!" I felt rather embarrassed because I suddenly realized that I was praying for each intention based on what I felt was best for each person and for each situation. I had never bothered to seek the Lord's will for those intentions. In all humility, I turned to the Lord and asked him, "Lord, what do *you* want *me* to pray for?"

At that point the Lord was able to teach me about the need to know his mind, will, and heart. I was already familiar with John 14:13: "Whatever you ask in my name, I will do." In fact, I had first become an intercessor precisely because I had prayed for several people and for several situations "in Jesus' name" and experienced his power at work. Encouraged by this initial success, I clutched this passage from Scripture and continued on in the ministry of intercession.

However, I realized that gradually I had lapsed into the habit of using Jesus' name as a mere formula to tack onto the end of my prayer. As I reflected on more recent results of my intercessory prayer at that time, I had to honestly admit to myself that what I was praying for was not happening. I turned to the Lord and prayed: "Lord, I know this word is truth. But from my experience, it doesn't work all the time. It seems very clear that the problem isn't with you, so the problem must be with me. Please help me to understand."

Almost immediately the Lord directed me to the passage in John 15:7, which was only about a page away from John 14:14: "If you abide in me and my words abide in you, ask whatever you will and it shall be done for you." I had read this passage many times before, but suddenly these words took on a new meaning. Here then, I thought, is the condition. God began to show me that the more I was immersed in his Word and lived in his Word and truth, the more I would understand his heart, mind, and will for each situation and grasp *his* priorities. In order to speak the name of Jesus, I needed to have an intimate association with him.

We have this intimate connection through baptism and confirmation, but it becomes alive in us as we abide in his Word and let his Word form us through his grace and the power of the Holy Spirit. The more we live in his Word, the more we know his mind. The more we know his mind, the more we can pray according to his will. At that point, whatever we ask in Jesus' name, he will do.

Attentive to God's Word

Unfortunately, oftentimes we are not very attentive to God's Word because of the many distractions that surround us. This is true at Mass, and it is also true during our private prayer time. If we are to truly know God's heart, mind, and will, we need to ask him to send us his Holy Spirit to enlighten our minds so that we might truly pray in his name. At the same time, we need to be vigilant when God's Word is proclaimed.

I had a rather unique experience in this regard when I was in Ghana, a country in West Africa, where I spoke at several conferences around the country. I was thrilled to be on my first visit to that country, yet I was starting to experience the fatigue that settles in whenever I travel.

It was time for Mass. I had no responsibilities during Mass, so it would have been easy to settle back and rest while the liturgy unfolded before me—especially during the Scripture readings and the homily! But when it came time for the Scripture readings, I witnessed a phenomenon that I have not seen elsewhere.

A man processed across a field that was about half the size of a football field, carrying the Word of God high above his head. A woman carrying a candle followed him. "The Word of God is light: light to your minds and light to your spirit," the commentator proclaimed.

Following the woman was another man. He carried a bowl of fire on his head, with the flames literally leaping out of the bowl. "The Word of God is like fire," the commentator proclaimed.

A young woman followed this man. She, too, was carrying a large bowl on her head, but her bowl was filled with water. As she processed across the field, she would pause and bow down, and some of the water would pour out of the bowl. "The Word of God is living water to our souls," the commentator announced.

Finally came a man carrying a two-edged sword. "The Word

of God is a two-edged sword separating bone from marrow," said the commentator. By this time I was truly ready to hear God's Word as it was proclaimed in the Scripture readings. I have carried the image of that procession with me ever since!

God's Word has the power to change our lives. As we get to know Christ, nothing in our lives will make any sense apart from him, whether it be friendships, conversations, or entertainment. It is important to realize that this is a process that continues throughout our lives. The more we conform our lives to God's Word through his grace, the more we will know his heart, mind, and will, and the more we will be able to ask in his name. With each passing day, we will see changes in the way we live, and we will experience more and more of God's power at work in us.

Of course, God often has to reduce us to nothing before we will truly rely on him and do what he wants us to do. If God is in the process of stripping you and pruning you, keep in mind that it is a process that leads to life. Thank him for it.

Remember His Word

Over the years I have had the privilege of getting to know many marvelous, holy people. Through my contact with them, I have often gained a glimpse of how they strive to make their home in Christ and let his Word take root in their lives.

Some years ago I had the tremendous experience of spending a day with Mother Teresa of Calcutta. She was the guest speaker for the graduation ceremony of the Franciscan University of Steubenville, and I was her hostess for the day.

During the course of the day I had various opportunities to ask her some questions. At one point I suddenly thought of the great wealth around us and the great waste that accompanies it. I felt somewhat chagrined because I knew that Mother Teresa spent most of her time working amid acute poverty. So I asked her, "Mother, you see all this wealth and all this waste. What is it like for you?"

She gave me a simple yet hard answer: "You know, when I'm at one of those banquets and they pass those big platters of meat down the table, I cannot help but think of my little ones scrabbling for a grain of rice that has fallen from the table. But then I remember Jesus' word to us: 'Never judge.' So I don't judge."

I was struck by Mother Teresa's response. Clearly she had read, studied, and pondered God's Word in all its simplicity, and she let it make its home in her heart. She was doing her utmost to conform her heart to his Word and to obey it. Look what it did for her and for the world!

Obedience to God's Word

On another occasion I heard the story of a Trappist monk, the abbot of a monastery in the United States for several years, who retired to a hermitage once his term of office was over. There he lived in prayer and solitude, except twice a week when a fellow monk would bring him some food.

Even though the monastery was located in a somewhat rural area, the drug and alcohol activity that plagues so much of this country extended even there. Two men (who must have been extremely drunk) broke into this monk's hermitage looking for money. Of course, the monk had no money, but the two men did not believe him and mercilessly beat him and left him for dead. By God's grace, the next morning was the appointed time for one of the semi-weekly food deliveries, so his fellow monk found him and took him to a hospital, where he miraculously recovered.

The sheriff found the two men who had assaulted the monk and brought them to the hospital for identification. But the monk informed the sheriff that he was not going to press charges. Needless to say, the sheriff was furious.

"Why not?" he asked.

The monk replied: "Because these two men gave me the greatest gift I've received in my life. They gave me the chance to identify with what the suffering of my Lord must have been like before he was hung on the cross. Nothing in my life makes sense apart from my conformity to Christ."

I do not want to imply that it would have been wrong for this monk to press charges in such a situation. A person can press charges and still forgive. In fact, in many situations like this, pressing charges might be the right thing to do—and the Christian thing to do. But God was not calling this monk to do so. God spoke into his ear and told him to set the whole matter totally aside. Even though it apparently made no sense to those around him, this monk heard God's word to him and was obedient to that word.

Pope John Paul II has been an inspiration to me, and I have been impressed by his obedience to God's word to him over the years. Throughout his life, for example, he has always had a special place in his heart for young people. As a young priest, he loved to work with youth. In fact, he was on a camping trip with a group of young people when he received word that he had been appointed a bishop. He confided to his close friends that being a bishop was not something that he wanted to do. Yet because he obeyed God's call to him he has ended up touching the hearts of millions of young people throughout his long pontificate. God has used him for his glory in a way that the young Bishop Wojtyla could never have imagined.

We need to obey and leave the results to God.

Deeper Union

There is an old story among the Desert Fathers. A young abbot asked an old abbot, "Father, I'm looking for wisdom. I keep my little rule. I keep the required fasts. I say my prayers daily. What more should I do?"

The old abbot lifted both hands up to heaven. His hands became like ten torches, and he replied, "Why not be totally changed into fire?"

Oftentimes we might feel that we are doing what is right and that we are doing everything we can do. We keep our fasts. We say our prayers. We try to do the best we can in the vocation the Lord has called us to. We might feel that there is little more that we can do. Yet we should remember the abbot's words as though they were words to us: "Why not be totally changed into fire?" In other words, let us just throw in our whole lot with the Lord and say, "God, I'm yours. Do with me what you want. Use me to reach many people. Use me to bring your word. Let my life be a sign of your presence."

The more we are united with Christ, the more we know God's will. What does God most want? Think of all the needs you have right now. Think of all the burdens that you are carrying in your heart. What is it that God most wants? God most wants people to give their lives to him and to know the power of his Holy Spirit. This is what God most desires.

So often when we pray, whether for ourselves or in intercession for others, our own ideas about what should be happening come rushing to the fore. (I know I'm repeating myself here, but listen...) We may think we are praying in Jesus' name, but in fact we do not stop to ask whether our requests actually represent what Jesus would want. I believe this is one of the primary reasons why so many people end up feeling that God does not answer their prayers. As the Letter of James says: "You ask and do not receive, because you ask wrongly, to spend it on your passions" (Jas 4:3).

Doing God's Work

Once I received a letter from a man who had attended a rally at which I spoke. He wrote that he, his wife, and his daughter stopped for dinner at a fast-food restaurant on their way home from the rally. When they arrived home, their daughter suddenly realized that she had left her purse at the restaurant.

She was devastated. The purse was a very expensive one that had been a special gift to her. Moreover, she had about a hundred dollars in cash in the purse. To top things off, she had taken off her jewelry—which was quite valuable—after the rally so she would be more comfortable for the ride home.

She had put it in her purse. Now the purse, the money, and the jewelry were gone. It was no small loss.

Her father immediately called the restaurant and asked the employees to search for the purse, but there was no sign of it. "We were angry and frustrated," he wrote. "Then I remembered your talk [about praying for what God wants]. So my wife, my daughter, and I came together and prayed that whoever took that purse would repent of their sin, give their life to the Lord, and come into the power of the Holy Spirit. This was the focus of our prayer."

Of course, the father was secretly hoping that whoever took the purse would also return it. Anxiously he called the restaurant on Monday, but there was no sign of the purse. He checked back on Tuesday, but no one had found it. "I was discouraged," he wrote. "I told myself that maybe God answers Sr. Ann Shields' prayers but not mine."

On Wednesday the manager of the restaurant called the family. They had the purse. When the family went to the restaurant to pick it up, the manager told them that he was absolutely dumbfounded: "I don't know where it came from. It was just sitting here on the table." They opened up the purse and discovered that everything was there. Nothing had been taken.

"We now have a commitment to keep praying for the person who took the purse. We're praying that whatever grace caused that person to return the purse will be completed, so that he or she will come into the fullness of life in Jesus Christ. We could have given in to our anger, frustration, and impatience, but God spoke." We could have focused only on our small need, but by God's grace, we didn't.

Jesus' promise, "If you ask anything of me in my name, I will do it," is made in the context of another promise, "He who believes in me will also do the works that I do" (Jn 14:12). Jesus' "works" have a very specific meaning in John's Gospel: they testify to his unity with the Father. "For whatever he does, that the Son does likewise," Jesus said. "These very works which I am doing bear me witness that the Father has sent me" (Jn 5:19, 36).

For us to do the works of Jesus means to do the work of his Father. It means bringing God's power into the world to save men and women from sin and death. And it is when we are doing the works of Jesus that we can trust that he will give us anything we ask.

CHAPTER 7

PRAYING FOR FAMILY AND NATION

We do not present our supplications before thee on the ground of our righteousness, but on the ground of thy great mercy. O Lord, hear; O Lord, forgive; O Lord, give heed and act; delay not, for thy own sake, O my God, because thy city and thy people are called by thy name.

DANIEL 9:18-19

The Old Testament as we read it today was born out of the most searing event in the history of ancient Israel: the destruction of Jerusalem in 587 B.C., followed by the exile of the Jews into Babylon. For almost two centuries the Jewish prophets had warned that judgment would befall God's people for their unfaithfulness to the covenant. Israel, the northern Jewish kingdom, was the first to fall; it was destroyed by the Assyrians in 721 B.C., and the ten northern tribes were scattered. The southern kingdom of Judah was spared for another hundred years, yet there also God's warnings were ignored.

What warnings had not accomplished, the humbling experience of God's judgment finally brought to pass. With no country, no capital city, and no temple, the Jews had to find a new identity as a people, an identity rooted only in their covenant with

God. Scribes gathered together the sacred books and oral traditions salvaged from the ruin of the temple to create a more organized record of God's law and his dealings with his covenant people. A great spiritual reformation began.

Throughout this long period of spiritual reform and testing, God's people raised a continual prayer of intercession for their nation, entreating the Lord for forgiveness, mercy, and restoration. We find many examples of intercessory prayer in the writings of the exile and post-exile period, including the prayers of Esther (see Esther 4:15-16), Nehemiah (see Nehemiah 1:5-11), Ezra (see Ezra 9:6-15), Baruch (see Baruch 1:15-3:8), and Daniel (see Daniel 9:3-19).

The predominant theme in these prayers is always one of confession and repentance: "Let thy ear be attentive, and thy eyes open, to hear the prayer of thy servant which I now pray before thee day and night for the people of Israel thy servant, confessing the sins of the people of Israel, which we have sinned against thee" (Neh 1:6). Even though these intercessors were often personally righteous and had not taken part in the nation's sin, they accepted responsibility for the guilt of their people.

Today we are witnessing a massive turning away from the Lord in societies that were once fundamentally Christian: the acceptance of abortion, the breakdown of sexual morality, the glorification of greed and selfishness. In these and so many other ways, God's people today are repeating the sins of ancient Israel.

Once again, God is warning us that sin and rebellion lead to judgment. He is calling us to repent, to confess our sins, to turn back to his ways. And he is calling us to intercede for our

Church and society, with the same attitude of personal responsibility that marked the great intercessors of the Old Testament. For this reason I feel that God entrusts two primary areas of intercession to those of us who feel called to this ministry: our families and our nation.

Praying for Our Families

It is easy to understand why God calls us in a particular way to become intercessors for our families. These are the people whom we love, and their needs and concerns become our needs and concerns through the intimate bond that we share with them.

When we look at the problems our families are facing, we can feel overwhelmed. At some point a typical family will face health problems, financial problems, and relationship problems—just to mention a few—that need prayer.

Indeed, these are some of the problems that we were facing in my own family some years ago. I was bringing these concerns to the Lord on a regular basis. As I prayed for these intentions, nothing seemed to happen. On the contrary, from all appearances things just seemed to get worse.

I turned to the Lord: "Can't I pray for these things, Lord? Isn't it your mind that people be healed and relationships be restored? Why do things seem to be taking a turn for the worse?" The Lord directed me to Matthew 6:25-33:

"Therefore I tell you, do not be anxious about your life, what you shall eat or what you shall drink, nor about your body, what you shall put on. Is not life more than food, and the body more than clothing? Look at the birds of the air: they neither sow nor reap nor gather into barns, and yet your heavenly Father feeds them. Are you not of more value than they? And which of you by being anxious can add one cubit to his span of life? And why are you anxious about clothing? Consider the lilies of the field, how they grow; they neither toil nor spin; yet I tell you, even Solomon in all his glory was not arrayed like one of these. But if God so clothes the grass of the field, which today is alive and tomorrow is thrown into the oven, will he not much more clothe you, O men of little faith? Therefore do not be anxious, saying, 'What shall we eat?' or 'What shall we drink?' or 'What shall we wear?' For the Gentiles seek all these things; and your heavenly Father knows that you need them all. But seek first his kingdom and his righteousness, and all these things shall be yours as well."

Kingdom Concerns

The message in this passage is rather simple. The Lord is telling us to bring whatever needs we have to him. He assures us that he will take care of them. But verse 33 particularly caught my attention because it seems to establish a priority: He will provide us with all our other *needs* only when *we seek first his kingdom and his way of holiness.*

At the time I was praying for a relative who was in serious difficulty, including drug and alcohol abuse. He had left home, and most people did not even know where he was. Whenever I prayed for him, I would ask the Lord to give him good friends, good counseling, or a good job. In fact, it had come to the point where my prayer for him consisted of a series of demands: "Lord, do this. Lord, do that." After I read this passage, I felt as though God suddenly put his hand over my mouth and said, "Seek first my kingdom for him, and all the other things he needs will be his as well."

So for the next year and a half this is what I did. It was hard because I wanted to pray for all his material needs. But I had to put first in my prayer what was first in God's prayer. I wanted and needed to pray *in Jesus' name.*

About a year and a half later my parents received a letter from this relative. They had not heard from him for eight or nine years. He wrote: "I know it must be a surprise to hear from me after all these years. But I want to thank you for standing by me. I want you to know that I've given my life to the Lord Jesus Christ. I want you to know that I've repented of my sin. I want you to know that I'm just about to be the father of a child. My wife and I together belong to this church, and we're really praying that we can raise our child according to God's Word."

God can change the life of your family if you put first in your heart what is first in God's heart. God certainly wants us to bring our human needs to him; he is honored when we do. But pray first of all and most of all for what God most wants.

When I spoke with this relative later on, I marveled at what God had done in his life. I realized that God's plan is so much better than our plan. I would have been satisfied if he had simply met good Christian friends, found a good job, and stayed off drugs and alcohol—a very human, limited vision. But God wanted him in his kingdom forever!

Praying for Repentance

After telling this story I began to hear from people who like-wise adjusted their prayers. They, too, were amazed at how quickly God answered their prayers.

One mother came up to me at a conference and told me that her son had been living with a woman for over three years outside of marriage. Needless to say, this arrangement caused immense anguish for her and her husband. They were very good Christian parents, and they prayed regularly that this arrangement would end, but nothing happened. In fact, both their son and the woman with whom he was living seemed to be growing increasingly comfortable with the arrangement, to the point where they were talking about permanently living together without the benefit of marriage.

"It was awful," this mother said. "Both his father and I were praying that God would do something, but nothing seemed to be happening. After I heard your talk, though, we changed the focus of our prayer. We started to pray that our son would be converted and come to know Jesus Christ and the power of the Holy Spirit. One month after we began to pray this way, our son called. 'Mom, I've broken off the relationship and I'd like to come back home. Can I?' he asked. I invited him over to talk to us about it.

"When he walked in the door, the first thing he told us was that he had been living in sin. I was flabbergasted. I didn't think my son even knew the word 'sin' let alone the meaning of it! He said that he knew he was wrong and that he wanted to change his life."

If you are a parent or a grandparent, an aunt or an uncle,

or a son or a daughter praying for a family member, pray according to the heart and Spirit of God. God knows everything about you. He knows the pain in your heart. He also knows your longings, hopes, and dreams. If you pray according to the heart and Spirit of God, he will not fail you. It may take years, but persevere. God will not silence you nor will he turn a deaf ear to your prayer.

When we get to heaven and stand before God on that glorious day, we do not want to suddenly realize how many other people we could have reached or touched through our words or prayers. We have to take advantage of every opportunity God extends to us. If we do so, our prayers will change the world. Praying with and for our families is the first step.

Praying for Our Nation

For many years now I have been increasingly aware of the grief and the pain that the Lord experiences as he looks upon our nation, which he has blessed more abundantly than any other nation of the world. More and more we, collectively, are "turning our backs" on God.

Since 1960 alone, violent crime in our nation has increased 560 percent. There is one murder every twenty-two minutes, a forcible rape every five minutes, an aggravated assault every twenty-eight seconds, and a robbery every forty-seven seconds.

Family life in our nation is increasingly under attack. Since 1960, divorce has quadrupled, teen suicide is up 200 percent, teenage abortions are up 1,000 percent, and the number of children raised in single-parent homes has tripled.

Economically, the national debt of the United States is now between four and five trillion dollars. (Do not tell me about economic surpluses. It is a matter of robbing Peter to pay Paul!) A property crime is committed every two seconds—33 percent of them by people under eighteen years of age.

When the Pope was speaking in America on one of his trips, he, too, recognized the spiritual battle in which we are engaged: "There is a battle on for the soul of this nation." We have turned away from God. The problem is neither a Republican problem nor a Democratic one. It is a sin problem. But the Lord is inviting us to repent and turn to him.

Getting Our Attention

All of these signs point to personal, family, corporate, and national loss of values based on Judeo-Christian principles. They are the fruit of rebellion, greed, anger, and hatred in our personal lives, our families, and our nation. We, as a nation and often as individuals, have forsaken God. We have rejected his lordship over us.

Even though we might be blind to the source of our moral collapse, God does not give up on us. He is giving us additional signs, hoping that we will see the error of our ways. In Matthew 16:1-4 we read:

The Pharisees and the Sadducees came, and to test him they asked him to show them a sign from heaven. He answered them, "When it is evening, you say, 'It will be fair weather; for the sky is red.' And in the morning, 'It will be stormy today, for the sky is red and threatening.' You know how to interpret the appearance of the sky, but you cannot interpret the signs of the times. An evil and adulterous generation seeks for a sign, but no sign shall be given to it except the sign of Jonah." So he left them and departed.

Jesus chides the Pharisees and the Sadducees because they are adept at interpreting some physical signs, such as the weather, but are oblivious to many other signs that surround them, particularly the signs and wonders that accompanied Jesus' ministry. "I'm speaking to you loudly," he was saying, "but you fail to read the signs around you."

For many years I have been paying close attention to the many physical signs that I see around us and making a sincere effort to understand them. I believe that God is trying to speak to us through the natural disasters that are increasing around the world.

Hurricanes have lashed our country at an unprecedented rate and intensity and have caused billions of dollars in damage. Tornadoes have also increased in intensity: one year there were more tornadoes in November than the combined total for the months of April and May, which are the traditional months for tornadoes.

Floods have devastated thousands of square miles of our land. At the same time, droughts have afflicted other areas of our country, causing billions of dollars in crop damage over the years. Blizzards have stricken areas that historically have received very little snow. A few years ago the East Coast witnessed the single biggest storm of the century, according to the National Weather Bureau, accompanied by more rain, sleet, hail, and snow than any storm since 1888.

Observing all this, I cannot help but ask myself, "Is God trying to get our attention?" My mother, who comes from a generation where faith is very private, came to me and said almost in a whisper, "Honey, is God trying to say something to us through these things?" The answer is clear: Yes, he is. Of course, there are human answers, such as El Niño in the Pacific and the greenhouse effect caused by pollution. However, these are merely human attempts to explain the chaos that surrounds us.

What Is God Saying?

But who is Lord of all creation? Who is the one who brought it into being? God himself created it and rules over it. Whatever God ordains or allows in his human creation or in his natural creation is there to speak to us.

Critics charge that this is an "Old Testament" concept that is now outdated. According to this line of reasoning, people back then were uneducated and superstitious. They did not comprehend the forces of nature, so they attributed everything to God.

I do not wish to belittle the theories and explanations that science has put forth. At the same time, I feel that we need to recognize that they are merely secondary causes. God is the Lord of all creation. Is not God speaking to us through these situations? Through the centuries has he not used his natural creation—floods, fires, earthquakes, and famines—to call us to repentance? Indeed, I believe God is saying, "Come back to me! The things you depend upon are not permanent. You cannot put your trust in them. Put your trust in me. Put your hope in me. Find life in me. Repent!"

Other critics claim that these natural catastrophes are not from God because God would not let the innocent suffer. I do not claim to understand the ways of God, but I do know Scripture. In Matthew 5:45 Jesus tells us that the Father in heaven "sends rain on the just and on the unjust." Blessings come to the righteous and the unrighteous; likewise, pain comes to the just and the unjust. We need to understand that God is not causing the innocent to suffer; our sins—rebellion, pride, and greed—are causing them to suffer. None of us is innocent; "all have sinned and fall short of the glory of God" (Rom 3:23).

God is pouring his grace upon us so we can respond as just men and women: "Lord, may you be glorified in trial as well as in blessing." May we be like Job, who could say, "Even though he slay me, yet will I trust him." May we be among those who can say, "The Lord is speaking to us and saying, 'Come back to me, America.'"

In 2 Chronicles 7:13-14, God appeared to Solomon and said: "When I shut up the heavens so that there is no rain, or command the locust to devour the land, or send pestilence among my people, if my people who are called by my name humble themselves, and pray and seek my face, and turn from their wicked ways, then I will hear from heaven, and will forgive their sin and heal their land."

I believe this is God's word to us today. If we will commit ourselves even more to a righteous life, if we will pray for our families and for our country in Jesus' name, God will hear our prayer and restore us.

Local Prayer

There are countless needs in our nation that we can pray for, and there are countless ways in which we can pray. It is always good to pray specifically that people will repent of the many sins that pervade our life and culture. It is especially good to pray for sinful situations in our local area.

For example, there is hardly a city today that does not have a busy abortion clinic. Fortunately, more and more Christians are regularly interceding for an end to this problem and are confronting it on a local level.

Several years ago three women contacted me after they attended a conference at which I spoke. "We had been praying for three months that an abortion clinic in our city would be closed, but nothing happened. Then we came to your talk. On the way home we asked ourselves, 'Are we praying in Jesus' name?' At first we all responded, 'Of course we are! Jesus would want that abortion clinic to close!'

"Then we grew increasingly uneasy. We began to ask the Lord to truly reveal his will to us. We sensed that we should adjust our prayer and pray that the owner of the clinic would be converted to Jesus. One month later the clinic closed."

Are you in tune with the heart of Jesus? He is always seeking to bring a sinner home to himself. He is mercy, and our prayer needs to reflect the heart of God.

When we persist in prayer and submit our prayer to God, our prayer will be answered. Often it will not be answered in the time frame that we have in mind, but God is still working in the hearts of those for whom we are praying.

One young man wrote that he had been praying for some

time that a pornographic theater in his town would close. "I prayed and prayed, but nothing happened," he recalled. "Then I heard you talk about those three women who were praying that the abortion clinic in their city would close, and how it closed once they started to pray for the conversion of its owner. That's my problem, I thought. I've got to pray for the conversion of the man who owns the theater. So I started to pray that way."

A week later, this young man was in his car at a traffic light, waiting for the light to change. He noticed a well-dressed businessman thumbing a ride on the side of the road, in front of his car. It was obvious that he had a flat tire.

"I leaned over, opened the door, and welcomed him into my car. Guess who he was—the owner of the theater! God put him right in my path! For what purpose? I know I'm supposed to pray. But I also know that I'm supposed to evangelize. I got his name, address, and phone number. Pray for me that I can do it."

From this example, it seems clear that sometimes God puts us to work when he answers our prayers! But again, do you see that God wants to bring his sons and daughters home? Sinful activities will die once hearts are changed!

Back in 1984 Los Angeles was chosen as the site for the summer Olympics. It was a great honor for the city, but there was a group of local people who were concerned for the safety of the thousands of people who would attend the games. Los Angeles has an average of seven murders on a given day, not to mention innumerable armed assaults on individuals.

So this group of intercessors went into the city and prayed for the protection of all those who would be competing and all those who would be visiting. They especially prayed that men and women would come to know the Lord Jesus Christ, recognize their sin, and repent of it. During the two weeks that the games took place, there was not a single murder recorded.

God wants to hear our prayer, and he wants to answer it. Sometimes he will work in response to our prayer, and sometimes he will put us to work.

We will, of course, be judged as individuals. But since we are part of a sinful society, oftentimes we will have to endure God's judgment on a sinful society. Since we are not perfect, occasionally we will contribute to society's sinfulness. In the midst of all the sin in us and all the sin in our nation, we need to turn to the Lord. God wants to hear our prayer. God wants us to be like watchmen on the ramparts who say: "Turn your eyes to the Lord. Repent of sin. Be ready!"

CHAPTER 8

LOVE YOUR NEIGHBOR

When the Pharisees heard that he had silenced the Sadducees, they came together. And one of them, a lawyer, asked him a question, to test him. "Teacher, which is the greatest commandment in the law?" And he said to him, "You shall love the Lord your God with all your heart, and with all your soul, and with all your mind. This is the great and first commandment. And a second is like it, You shall love your neighbor as yourself. On these two commandments depend all the law and the prophets."

MATTHEW 22:34-40

Our call as intercessors does not stop with our families, our church, or even our nation. As members of God's people, we are called to be intercessors for all of humanity—in fact, for all creation. In Romans 8:19 St. Paul reminds us: "The creation waits with eager longing for the revealing of the sons of God."

Scripture explicitly calls us to pray for all people. And the reason is very simple: God loves all people. God did not send his Son to the world just to save a small band of chosen disciples or even those fortunate enough to become Christians in the ensuing centuries. God wants all people everywhere to come to salvation through his Son Jesus Christ.

Our Call as Disciples

As followers of Jesus, we share a serious responsibility for the rest of the world. For one thing, we are called to evangelization, announcing the good news of Jesus to the end of the earth. But we are also called to intercession, for it takes prayer as well as preaching to open the doors of the human heart so evangelization can be effective.

The apostle Paul understood this truth, and his letters often request intercessory prayer to support his ministry as an apostle announcing the Gospel: "And pray for us also, that God may open to us a door for the word, to declare the mystery of Christ" (Col 4:3). In another letter Paul wrote: "Finally, brethren, pray for us that the word of the Lord may speed on and triumph, as it did among you" (2 Thes 3:1). And again, "[Pray] also for me, that utterance may be given me in opening my mouth boldly to proclaim the mystery of the gospel" (Eph 6:19).

In recent years much of the Church has lost that missionary zeal for spreading the gospel. Instead we hear people saying, "Don't impose your beliefs on others"; "One religion is as good as another"; "It doesn't matter what people believe, as long as they believe in something." These attitudes effectively deny the uniqueness of the gospel as the only truth that can lead to salvation. If we are sincerely concerned about the people of the world, if we share God's love for them and God's desire that all be saved, we cannot keep the truth of the gospel to ourselves. We must proclaim it—both as individuals, sharing the good news of Jesus with people around us, and as a Church, taking the message to the ends of the earth.

If this is to happen, we need to grow not only in love of God but also in love of our neighbor—or the virtue of charity. Often we think that charity means what we give to the poor or the services that we render to other people. These are certainly external expressions of charity, but they are not the heart of charity. The heart of charity is what happens inside me through Baptism. It is my "walking" in union with God, who is love, and recognizing his presence in my neighbor. Charity is obedience to the second great commandment to love one another as he has loved us. The two great commandments cannot be separated.

In my community's care for medically fragile children, I find it easy to love the babies with all my heart. But there are times when the older children will do something that makes it hard for me to love them. In these situations I realize that my love is very limited. However, God's love is not limited, and I need to remind myself of this. The heart of charity is that I surrender my life in such a way that God's love can work through me.

Jesus reminds us of this in John 13:35: "By this all men will know that you are my disciples, if you have love for one another."

Forgive One Another

God never commands us to do something without giving us the power to do it. Unfortunately, we often have a hard time accepting God's mandate to us. If someone hurts us or offends us, either in a small way or a great way, we often say, "I might forgive them if they come to me on their knees and acknowledge how terribly they've hurt me." Essentially, we end up refusing to forgive and holding these people in spiritual debt to us.

In Matthew 18:21 Peter asks Jesus how many times he should forgive his brother when his brother sins against him. Jesus responds by telling him the parable of the unmerciful servant.

This is the parable about a king who wanted to settle accounts with his servants. One of his servants owed him a large sum of money but was unable to pay. The king told him that he, his wife, his children, and his possessions would all be sold in order to repay the debt.

The servant fell on his knees before his master and pleaded for mercy. "Lord, have patience with me," he begged, "and I will pay everything." The servant's master had pity on him, canceled the debt, and let him go.

Just as soon as this servant was released, he went to one of his fellow servants who owed him some money. He grabbed him and began to choke him. "Pay what you owe," he demanded. But his fellow servant was unable to pay back the money. He, too, pleaded for mercy, but the servant took no pity on him. Instead, he had him thrown into prison until he could repay his debt.

The king found out what had happened and summoned the servant in. "You wicked servant!" he said. "I forgave you all that debt of yours because you besought me, and should not you have had mercy on your fellow servant, as I had mercy on you?" The king turned the servant over to the jailers to be tortured until he paid back everything he owed. "So also my heavenly Father will do to every one of you, if you do not forgive your brother from your heart," Jesus warns us.

No hurt nor any offense is impossible to forgive—by God's grace and dependence upon him moment by moment. Remember what happened to Jesus even though he was totally innocent. What was his response? From the cross, in the midst of horrendous pain, he said, "Father, forgive them; for they know not what they do" (Lk 23:34). We are called to love as he loves and power will be given us to be like Jesus.

If we are harboring resentment, revenge, envy, or jealousy, and if our hearts are cold and hard, do you think we will pray effectively? Do you think God will hear our prayer? Ongoing growth in living out the two great commandments is at the foundation of our life as intercessors.

The Mexican Martyrs

On May 21, 2000, Pope John Paul II canonized twenty-five Mexican martyrs who died during the *Cristero* Rebellion in Mexico during the 1920s and 1930s. During this period in Mexican history, the ruling party in Mexico made several attempts to eradicate the Catholic Church in that country. The persecution that the government unleashed was fierce: Church property was confiscated, seminaries were closed, foreign priests were barred from the country, and severe restrictions were imposed on priests and nuns.

Some Catholics, feeling that they had no other choice, took up arms in an effort to restore their religious liberty. They were known as the *Cristero* rebels. Eventually, a truce was negotiated with the government, although anti-Catholic legislation remained in effect until almost the end of the century. The

Cristero Rebellion left an indelible mark on Mexican history, and even today people there recall the battle cry of the *Cristeros: Viva Cristo Rey!*

When Pope John Paul II canonized these martyrs, he held them up for our example. They truly epitomize what it means to love and forgive. For example, Fr. Jenaro Sanchez, the pastor of a parish in Tecolotlan, Jalisco, was arrested and hanged from a mesquite tree. When the soldiers put the rope around his neck, he said, "My countrymen, you are going to hang me, but I pardon you, and my Father God pardons you, and long live Christ the King!"

Another priest, Fr. Julio Alvarez, pastor of a church in Mechoacanejo, Jalisco, was arrested, tied to the saddle of a horse, and led away to Leon. There he was sentenced to death. On hearing his sentence he said, "I know that you have to kill me because you are ordered to do so, but I am going to die innocent because I have done nothing wrong. My crime is to be a minister of God. I pardon you." He then crossed his arms, and the soldiers fired their guns. They threw his body onto a trash heap near the church.

Where does such love—love expressed by forgiveness—come from if not from the heart of Christ?

Anacleto Gonzalez Flores was a fiery young attorney from Tepatitlan, Jalisco, who pledged to use his oratorical talents in service to God and his country. A social activist for many years, he was taken prisoner at the outset of the *Cristero* Rebellion. He was tortured in the government's effort to learn more about the *Cristeros*. His captors hanged him by his thumbs until they were dislocated; they slashed the bottoms of his feet. Yet Flores refused to give any information. Finally he was executed.

Thousands of people filed by Flores' casket to pay their final respects. His widow brought their two young sons into the room where their father's body lay. "Look," she said to her eldest son. "This is your father. He has died defending the faith. Promise me on his body that you will do the same when you are older if God asks it of you." What faith this woman had! This was not a time for revenge, bitterness, hardness of heart, or despair. On the contrary, it was a time to call her children on in the faith.

We need to beg God for this same faith. We need to beg him for the grace to live the same kind of righteous, loving life, no matter the cost.

A Living Witness

As I have traveled around the world over the past few years, I have heard many remarkable testimonies. Particularly inspiring are some stories of people—many still living, others only recently deceased—who have manifested a tremendous capacity to love God and to love their neighbor.

When Pope John Paul II celebrated the fiftieth anniversary of his ordination to the priesthood, he invited a Jesuit priest, Fr. Anton Luli from Albania, to be the homilist at the solemn vesper service that was part of the celebration. Fr. Luli was in his eighties at the time. He told those present that he was reluctant to share his testimony; he was doing so only out of obedience.

Shortly after Fr. Luli was ordained to the priesthood in 1946, a communist dictatorship took over Albania. Thus began a period of ruthless persecution that continued for over forty years. Some of Fr. Luli's confreres died as martyrs after a trial of lies and deceit. But Fr. Luli was not among them: "Instead, the Lord asked me to live. Opening my arms and letting myself be nailed to the cross, thus I celebrated my Eucharist, my priestly offering in the ministry denied me, with a life spent in chains and every kind of torture."

Fr. Luli was arrested on December 19, 1947. He spent the next seventeen years in solitary confinement. After that, he spent many more years in a forced labor camp.

"My first prison in that freezing month of December was a lavatory in a village in the mountains of Shkodër," Fr. Luli recalled. "I stayed there for nine months, forced to crouch on hardened excrement and never being able to stretch out because the space was so small.

"On Christmas night they dragged me from that place and put me in another lavatory, on the second floor of the prison. They forced me to strip and hung me up with a rope passed under my arms. I was naked and could barely touch the ground with the tips of my toes. I felt my body slowly and inexorably failing me. The cold gradually crept up my limbs, and when it reached my breast and my heart was about to give in, I gave a desperate cry. My torturers arrived; they pulled me down and kicked me all over. That night, in that place and in the solitude of that first torture, I experienced the real meaning of the Incarnation and the cross.

"But in this suffering, I had beside me and within me the comforting presence of the Lord Jesus, the Eternal High Priest. At times his support was something I can only call 'extraordinary,' so great was the joy and comfort he communicated to me.

"But I have never felt resentment for those who, humanly speaking, robbed me of my life. After my release I happened to meet one of my torturers in the street: I took pity on him; I went toward him and embraced him."

Fr. Luli was released in the amnesty of 1989, when the communist regime finally fell. He had been in prison for forty-two years.

A Mother Finds Peace

Another story that made a deep impression on me is that of a woman named Marietta Jaeger-Lane. Twenty-six years ago Marietta's then seven-year-old daughter, Susie, was kidnapped and murdered in Montana. Needless to say, Marietta was filled with bitter sadness, anger, and all-consuming rage. She was ready to pounce on the person who had killed her precious child.

As time went on, however, a transformation took place in Marietta's life. "I basically had two choices: either let anger and hostility devour me, or adopt a more Christian outlook," she recalled. Marietta chose to open her heart to God. As she did so, she began to experience God's compassion and mercy.

On the first anniversary of her daughter's abduction, the telephone rang. It was Susie's assailant. Still at large, the man who later was proven to be Susie's killer called Marietta to taunt and torment her, hoping to cause even more pain and suffering. Instead, he discovered a calm and caring Christian woman who was reaching out and offering healing to his tormented soul.

"He was totally undone by my demeanor and attitude," Marietta explained. "In fact, he was so completely caught off guard that he stayed on the phone long enough and revealed things about himself that made it possible for the FBI to identify and apprehend him."

However, Susie's murderer later escaped. Once again he called Marietta to taunt her and intimidate her. But she once again extended her calm Christian demeanor.

"During this conversation I called him by his name," Marietta remembers. "Taken aback by my friendliness, he incriminated himself again and revealed his whereabouts. This time there would be no escape."

Marietta was able to meet her daughter's killer. "He was suspected of being a serial killer, but he would not confess to any murders," Marietta recalls. "Montana had a death penalty statute that was in effect in 1974, but I asked the prosecutors not to impose it in this case. I wanted them to seek a mandatory life sentence instead. They agreed, and in my meeting with Susie's killer, I was able to convince him to confess to the crime. He never did confess to other murders that carried a death sentence penalty."

Since that time Marietta has worked extensively with various organizations that help the families of murder victims. "In all of my experiences, I've discovered that the death penalty simply does not heal families traumatized by murder. Hate destroys; it does not heal. And it is healing that these families need," Marietta says. "I did not want my daughter's legacy to be defined by revenge through the death penalty. She was too beautiful and too sweet for that."

Some people would call Marietta a fool. Some people

would call her stupid. But God calls his disciples to walk in the Master's footsteps. Leave the punishment to him. Are we generous enough to open our hearts to forgive even when people are not asking for forgiveness? Are we generous enough to forgive even when they do not know the extent to which they have hurt us? Are we willing to forgive even when they do not care? Are we willing to tell them that we forgive them and, no matter what their response, we will keep our hearts open and pray that God will convert them and bless them? We can only do this by God's grace.

Love Amid Grief

A few years ago two young men, students at the Franciscan University of Steubenville living in off-campus housing, were abducted from their house and tragically murdered. The mother of one of those young men publicly forgave the murderers even before her son's body was found. Later she established a scholarship fund in her son's name for inner-city youth. In a letter to the grandmother who had raised one of the boys implicated in the murder, she acknowledged that they both were suffering unbearable grief, that they both had, in a certain sense, lost children. She promised to pray for the grandmother in her sorrow. Where does such strength come from if not from the Lord?

In 1999 the nation was shocked when two young teenagers went on a killing rampage at their high school in Littleton, Colorado. A number of students were shot dead, and several others severely injured. At one point the young men confronted young Cassie Bernall and asked her whether she believed in God. When she professed her faith, they shot her dead.

Later Cassie's mother wrote: "We are both proud and in great pain. Her death remains unbearable. And yet I have a lot of years left in this world without Cassie. I don't want to be bitter. I do not want to be angry. God does give you the grace if you open up to it."

The parents of Dylan Klebold, one of the boys who murdered those young people, wrote to the Bernalls expressing their grief and sorrow for them and for Cassie's death. Mrs. Bernall said, "My husband and I wrote back to them and said we have both lost children. Let us pray for one another."

Where does this Christian attitude come from? Where does the strength come from? When I reflect on all the little slights and little injuries that I suffer, I am ashamed when I realize how often they leave me bent out of shape. We have to examine our consciences regularly. Are we holding on to any hurts or resentments? It does not help to hold on to them; they only harden our hearts and make us bitter. We have to learn how to forgive and leave any punishment in the hands of God. This is one of the deepest expressions of love, and it is at the heart of the virtue of charity: "Love one another as I have loved you."

Love Your Enemy

Not too long ago I read a story in the newspaper about a young Christian man named Steve who lived in Pennsylvania, not too far from where I grew up. He was appalled to read a newspaper article one day about an abortion clinic that was opening up in his town. As Steve was reading the article, he felt that the Lord was telling him to pray for the owner of the clinic, who was quoted in the article. He put the paper down and dismissed the thought. But the next day he sensed that the Lord was telling him that he needed to love the owner of that clinic.

Steve was somewhat at a loss as to how he might express love for the owner of the clinic. So he decided that he would just go and stand outside the abortion clinic and pray. Soon the owner emerged. He was considerably bigger than Steve—about six-foot-four and weighing close to three hundred pounds. He took advantage of his size to try and intimidate Steve. He screamed in his face and told him to go away. But Steve just looked at him until he went back into the clinic.

Steve returned to the clinic every day. Each time he would just stand there and pray. Often the owner would emerge and shout at him, but Steve just stood there and prayed.

One day the owner asked Steve what he wanted.

"Your peace," Steve replied.

"Listen, I'm fine. Everything's fine. I don't need you," the owner told him.

Steve did not know that four months earlier the owner's mother and sisters had confronted him about his business. His visit with them had left him troubled. On his way home he had shouted out to God, "I don't even know if you exist, but if you do exist and if I'm doing something wrong, send someone to help me."

Steve also did not know that each day as he stood in front of that abortion clinic, the owner went down the hall and pulled back the blinds to gaze at Steve's face. He later explained that he was drawn to the love that was reflected in that face. No one had ever loved him like that.

In his final confrontation with Steve, the owner shouted, "What are you doing here anyway?"

"I'm here as an answer to your prayer," Steve replied. (Only God could have revealed this to Steve!)

Today the abortion clinic is closed. The owner is now a committed Christian. Why? First, Steve heard God and obeyed him. Secondly, Steve prayed for the owner and put his own life on the line. Later Steve even invited him for dinner and bowling with Steve's family.

When you start to pray, God may ask you to do certain things. God is calling us to love those with whom we would ordinarily not relate. God is asking us to pour out our lives for those from whom we would normally stay away. God is pouring out his love for his people, and he wants to use you and me. Are you ready to obey?

God's Grace Is at Work!

This is a *kairos* moment, a season of grace. It is time to open our hearts to the Lord, asking him to replace our stony hearts with hearts of flesh. We have to ask him for the grace and courage to let go of hurts and resentments. We have all been hurt by others—sometimes very badly and very tragically—but when we open our hearts to forgive, the river of grace flows in to wash us clean.

Suppose we can only say, with clenched teeth and fists, "I

forgive. I'll try to let go." Something far greater goes on in the heavens. We unleash spiritual power to defeat the enemy. Even if we start reluctantly, God will still come with grace and with power.

If you want your intercession for your family, for the nation, and against the evils in our society to be heard, take God's Word to heart. Start with one thing that you know God is asking you to do that you are not doing. "I'm doing six other things!" you might protest. "Isn't that enough?" Yet we need to keep opening up our hearts. This is how saints are made. God may have a lot in store for us that will affect the whole world. Our willingness to follow the Lord unleashes spiritual power and grace, so that we can affect many people in our lives as intercessors.

CHAPTER 9

FURTHER EQUIPMENT FOR THE BATTLE

When I began this book, I spoke specifically of the grace and power of the sacraments, not simply as ceremonies and blessings for the day but as a sharing of God's own life to equip us to live the Christian life. As we draw these teachings to a close, I want to comment on other gifts from God that can help us become more effective intercessors.

Timeless Devotions

We all know the value of prayer in the life of an intercessor. Let us not overlook some of the beautiful prayers and devotions that have been around for many years. They are valuable instruments in the life of an intercessor.

The rosary is an especially powerful prayer of intercession. Consider the words of the Hail Mary: "Holy Mary, Mother of God, pray for us sinners now and at the hour of our death." We are asking Mary, who was so specially favored by God and who occupies a unique place in heaven, to intercede for us. We ask her to pray for us now, with our human and earthly needs, and at the hour of our death, that we might fulfill the purpose for which we were created. What greater eternal perspective could a prayer have?

Mother Teresa of Calcutta was a great advocate of intercession through devotional prayer. One of her favorite prayer devotions was one that she "stumbled" across as she grew in holiness. She called it an "express novena." Most novenas are designed for prayer over a nine-day or nine-week period. But Mother Teresa was often confronted with many pressing needs that had to be resolved rather quickly. She would pray the *Memorare*, a beautiful and popular prayer to the Blessed Mother that many of us use. But when in great need, Mother Teresa would pray it nine times in a row!

Back in the 1980s Mother Teresa obtained permission from the communist regime in East Germany to open a convent in East Berlin, so that her sisters could begin their charitable work there. In 1988 the superior of her convent there suddenly became very ill and had to return to India. Mother had to send another sister to take her place. When she requested a visa for the new superior, the East German government said that it would take six months to process the application. Mother told them she could not wait six months; the ill sister had to return to India, and a replacement was essential.

In the midst of the seeming impasse, Mother summoned her sisters to the chapel. There they began to pray the "express novena." When they were praying the *Memorare* for the eighth time, the telephone rang. It was an official from the Foreign Ministry who simply wanted to reiterate that it would take six months to process the sister's visa application. So Mother returned to the chapel, and all prayed the ninth *Memorare*. Then there was silence.

At that point Mother Teresa prayed out in a way that only someone who was totally conformed to God's will could dare to pray: "Mary, we have prayed this novena with confidence. You have not seen fit to answer yet. So we will begin again." What persistence!

The sisters began to pray the novena a second time. Once again the telephone rang during the eighth *Memorare.* It was the Foreign Ministry, informing Mother Teresa that the visa would be delivered the next day.

Remember: *Nothing* is "magic." There are no formulas. What we are always talking about in intercession and most especially in this example is the fruit of a relationship. We are, above all, sons and daughters of God, and we can always come with confidence to our Father. The more we are willing to be conformed to his will in our lives and prayer, the more we can see the results of our intercession.

Fasting

Fasting is another holy practice that is well suited to intercession. In the Old Testament the prophet Daniel expressed his prayer of intercession in actions as well as words: "Then I turned my face to the Lord God, seeing him by prayer and supplications with fasting and sackcloth and ashes." (Dn 9:3).

Sackcloth and ashes were signs of mourning in the ancient world; they were also used to express repentance and sorrow for sin. We Catholics still receive ashes at the beginning of each Lent to express repentance for sin and willingness for greater conversion. Yet in most circumstances, sackcloth and ashes would be more distracting than prayerful in the presence of others.

Fasting, however, remains a very important form of intercession and prayer. As a form of personal penance and self-denial, fasting expresses our repentance for sin. Thus it is particularly appropriate when we are interceding about our own rebellion and unfaithfulness and that of God's people.

Fasting also expresses our commitment to intercession. "I am really serious. I want to pray, Lord, for this person or for this situation. As I deny my own will through fasting, give me a greater openness to your will, to your purpose in allowing this situation."

Practically, I believe the time-honored Christian practice of observing one fast day each week can provide a powerful opportunity for intercession. The type of fast that a person chooses to follow can vary according to one's age, health, and work. Some may omit a favorite food or beverage; others may skip one or all meals; still others may consume only bread and water.

Consider the place this holy practice should have in your life. Be honest about what you believe God is asking of you in the way of fasting. You can open a powerful avenue for intercession.

Pray in the Spirit

The Holy Spirit invaded the Catholic Church about thirty years ago in a new way. The practice of praying in tongues, popularized by that movement, is probably one of the best ways to turn our prayer over to the Holy Spirit and let him pray within us.

Many theologians agree that this was what St. Paul was referring to when he wrote: "Likewise the Spirit helps us in our weakness; for we do not know how to pray as we ought, but the Spirit himself intercedes for us with sighs too deep for words" (Rom 8:26). Elsewhere St. Paul wrote, "For one who speaks in a tongue speaks not to men but to God; for no one understands him, but he utters mysteries in the Spirit" (1 Cor 14:2).

Praying in tongues provides a very clear experience of the Holy Spirit's praying through us. The gift of tongues is first a gift of worship. Through tongues we yield to the Holy Spirit within us who is constantly worshipping the Father through us. Remember, by Baptism you are a temple of the Holy Spirit. It is real. Tongues is one sign of that reality.

Those who have never exercised this gift of the Holy Spirit might find some other form of wordless prayer helpful. Simply being quiet before the Lord can be a form of prayer in the Spirit. But also consider asking the Lord for the gift of tongues. Just open your heart and let the Spirit do the praying!

Help From the Saints

Finally, consider the role of the Church triumphant in our intercession. Most likely we can all recall times when we have benefited from the prayers of a loving parent, friend, or relative. We experience a tremendous loss when these people die. Do they no longer care about our well-being once they have gone to be with the Lord? Would God be offended if we asked them to intercede for us?

Clearly we all participate in the one mediation of Jesus Christ. When the first martyrs died, their fellow Christians recognized them as heroes of the faith and held them to be in

God's presence, glorious in God's sight. At first the early Christians reverently preserved their relics and celebrated the anniversary of their death each year. It was only a short step then to seek their help and prayers since they were now with Christ in glory.

Indeed, many holy men and women over the ages recognized the fact that their most important work lay ahead, beyond the grave. When St. Dominic was dying, he consoled his brothers by telling them, "Do not weep, for I shall be more useful to you after my death, and I shall help you then more effectively than during my life." Likewise, St. Thérèse of Lisieux wrote, "I want to spend my heaven doing good on earth."

There are many traditional prayers and novenas that we can use to call upon the saints in heaven. These men and women, already closely united to Christ, are in a good position to help us all grow in holiness. They never cease to intercede with the Father for us. Furthermore, they proffer the merits that they themselves acquired on earth through Jesus Christ, the one mediator between God and man. Out of their love for us and their fraternal concern, they are able to help us in our weakness.

Help From a Holy Woman

Many people have told me of the blessings they have received over the years through the intercession of those who have gone before us. One such story concerns a young man named Andy.

Andy was quite difficult as a child. At first his parents were not overly concerned, but things got worse. In fourth grade he was diagnosed with learning disabilities, which made him feel dumb and angry. He stopped caring. By the time he was thirteen, he was hanging out with a wild crowd.

Andy's mother had been raised in a strong Christian family, and she tried to instill the same values in her three sons. The other two sons responded well, but Andy did not. Day in and day out she continued to pray for Andy, begging God to send help.

Finally Andy was sent to a juvenile home. His words to his mother resounded in her mind as she walked away from visiting him: "I hate you, and I don't ever want to see you again." She was crushed emotionally, yet in a certain way relieved. Andy had started to talk about killing himself, and she knew that in the home he would be under constant surveillance.

After several agonizing months of negative reports and meetings, Andy began responding to therapy. In fact, his counselors told his parents that his progress was incredible. One day Andy called home: "Hi, Mom. I miss you. How are you?" Even in those few words she recognized, as only a mother can, that there was no anger, only respect. Some months later Andy came home for good. In his eyes his mother saw what she had not seen for years: joy.

"I felt grateful for the treatment center, assuming that they had worked magic," she said, "and in many ways they had."

A year later, though, Andy's mother discovered that he had received some extra help. One evening, as the whole family sat around relaxing together, Andy shared a dream he had had in the juvenile home: He was walking down a dirt road and came to an old house. An elderly woman sat on the porch reading her Bible. She was short and stout and had her white hair tied in a bun. She had beautiful blue eyes, Andy recounted. She wore a white shawl with a pattern on it like diamonds.

"I told her I was thirsty and she looked at me and said, 'Andy, you're going the wrong way.'" Once again he asked for water and she replied: "Andy, turn around. Change your ways." Andy said that when he woke the next morning he didn't feel angry. "The dream stays with me."

By this time Andy's mother was in tears. Unknowingly Andy had described his great-grandmother's front porch and the road that led to the house. He had given an accurate physical description of her as she was shortly before her death, a month before Andy was born—and Andy had never seen a picture of her beyond her thirtieth birthday. Andy's mother had inherited the diamond-patterned shawl. It had been in a trunk all those years; Andy had never seen it. (Adapted from *Chicken Soup for the Christian Soul*, Health Communications, 1997)

The Upward Call

Since we are surrounded by so great a cloud of witnesses, let us lay aside every weight, and sin which clings so closely, and let us run with perseverance the race that is set before us, looking to Jesus the pioneer and perfecter of our faith, who for the joy that was set before him endured the cross, despising the shame, and is seated at the right hand of the throne of God. Consider him who endured such hostility against himself, so that you may not grow weary or fainthearted.

HEBREWS 12:1-3